THE PERSONAL FREEDOM MANIFESTO

A NON-CONFORMIST'S GUIDE TO DISCOVERING YOUR
GREATNESS AND CREATING THE LIFE YOU WANT

DEDICATION

To my parents.
Thanks for all your love and support.

GET IN TOUCH

I love hearing from my readers, so feel free to get in touch. Whether you have a question, feedback or something you want to discuss, I look forward to hearing from you. Connect here;

www.escapethesystemnow.com

Email: joe@escapethesystemnow.com

Instagram: escapethesystem19

Twitter: escape_system19

YouTube: EscapeTheSystem

CONTENTS

INTRODUCTION 1

PART 1: BREAKING FREE 6

CHAPTER 1: GUIDANCE FOR LIVING AN EXTRAORDINARY LIFE 9

CHAPTER 2: FREE YOUR MIND SO YOU CAN ACHIEVE THE IMPOSSIBLE 23

CHAPTER 3: CHALLENGE THE 9 TO 5 TO FIND SOMETHING GREATER 43

CHAPTER 4: EMBRACE YOUR INDIVIDUALITY AND SHINE 60

PART 2: DISCOVERING YOUR GREATNESS 73

CHAPTER 5: CHANGE YOUR THOUGHTS TO CHANGE YOUR LIFE 75

CHAPTER 6: VITAL SKILLS TO BECOME OUTSTANDING....................................... 94

CHAPTER 7: DAILY PRACTISES FOR PEAK PERFORMANCE 107

CHAPTER 8: STRENGTHEN YOUR SPIRIT TO OVERCOME ANY CHALLENGE..... 125

PART 3: CREATING THE LIFE YOU WANT 138

CHAPTER 9: ADVICE FOR WHEN BEGINNING YOUR JOURNEY.......................... 141

CHAPTER 10: ESSENTIAL KNOWLEDGE FOR ACHIEVING RESULTS.................. 170

CHAPTER 11: PRACTICAL TIPS AND STRATEGIES FOR GETTING YOUR WORK NOTICED (AND MORE) 183

CHAPTER 12: CLARITY WHEN YOU FEEL LIKE EVERYTHING IS LOST 209

CONCLUSION: THE 5 STEPS TO FREEDOM 224

YOUR FREE GIFT 234

COACHING 238

ACKNOWLEDGEMENTS... 240

ENDNOTES 241

INTRODUCTION

If you've read any of my previous work, be it books, blog posts or even watched my YouTube videos or attended my talks, you'll know I'm passionate about letting people know they have options. You don't have to accept the life you are presented with. If you want something more, or different, it's within your power to create it.

If you're familiar with my work, you'll also know I'm fond of misquoting Henry David Thoreau. In his book *Waldon*, he stated that, "Most men lead lives of quiet desperation." Over the years, this quote has been embellished. Some wise soul added the words, "and go to the grave with the song still in them."

For me, this improves on Thoreau's insightful observation. Yes, the majority of people living in the so-called developed world are desperate. Mental health medication rates and suicide figures reveal this. Divorce is also an indication of our malaise. Even our inability to sleep (two thirds of the adult UK population report experiencing disrupted sleep[1]) reveals that something is amiss.

We're not happy with modern living. Its fast pace, polluted space, endless written and unwritten rules and various forms of media distractions, disconnect us from nature, our fellow man and the deeper calling of our inner selves. However, rather than protest this malaise, as Thoreau suggests, we suffer in silence.

Why does this happen? Why won't anyone speak out?

The simple answer is that we believe *we* are wrong for feeling the way we do. Since childhood, we've been conditioned to accept the world as it is presented. If we ever complain about the stifling limitations imposed upon us, we're told, "This is how the world works."

The implication behind this statement is life could never be any other way. Therefore, we are left in a predicament whereby we must adapt ourselves to the world. If we were to protest, we would be laying ourselves open to looking stupid and courting ridicule. Why challenge the unchallengeable? Far better to get on with life and make the best of what you've got.

This is why our desperation is "quiet." Voicing it appears pointless. Instead, we suffer in silence and attempt to finish the job society started by telling ourselves that we should,

- be happy with a boring job that offers little more than a monthly pay check.
- tolerate a lack of free time and never getting to do what we want.
- accept a passionless marriage devoid of intimacy.
- ignore our increasingly failing health as we prematurely age and deteriorate.

We should accept all of these things because that's what "good people" do. They get on with things, think about others and don't complain (or only complain behind closed doors). However, try as we might to force ourselves to fit into the narrow confines of what society wants us to be, the unease and desperation never leaves.

What is the impact of living in a state of "quiet desperation?" Sadly, we shut ourselves down. We trade passion and meaning for security and comfort. As a result, all that we could have been goes to the grave without ever being expressed.

This begs the question, what could you do with your life? What is your song? Could you have a positive impact on the world through a unique message you need to share? Might you have the potential to entertain millions, bringing joy and amusement into their life? Or, might you make a discovery that will save lives? These are all possibilities. However, they are only possibilities when you open your mind to the idea that *you are right* to want something more (or different).

Giving yourself permission to "want more" may sound selfish. It's the antithesis of what we've been taught. According to society, you should put others first, be humble and realistic. This makes you a reasonable and likeable person. On the other hand, those that "want more," or something different, are either selfish or troublemakers. However, despite avoiding these labels, and living with the *appearance* of being a good person, your soul will not thank you.

Try as you might to be what other people want, there will always be a part of you longing to be itself. The only way to free this part, and end the internal turmoil, is to embrace your desires. Go for what you want. Don't be restrained by society's notions of achievability or acceptability. By doing so, not only will you get to express your "song," you'll also have the potential to inspire others.

The rest of this book teaches you how to do this. The method I've chosen to achieve this aim is telling stories. You'll find that some of the sections are based on my personal experiences and most use examples taken from historical, and current, figures and various informative books or studies. Around each story, a lesson is offered, giving you the insight needed to get closer to creating the life you want.

What will this life look like? That's up to you to decide. I can't know the individual nuances of your desires. However, what I do know, is that you'll find your guidance within.

Within you, is an untapped well of ideas, visions and urges, all pushing you in the direction of greater creativity, fun, love and enjoyment. Tap into these. Use them to start piecing together a future where you set your own schedule, have the financial freedom to do the work you enjoy, have time for your hobbies and exercise, can travel when you feel like experiencing something new and have meaningful relationships that enrich your life. This is your aim and it's perfectly achievable with a combination of the knowledge in this book and your will to use it.

When putting it to use, you may prefer to read from cover to cover or dip into specific sections. If you're reaching the end of your resolve, and considering giving up, you can scroll to the back of the book and discover the three questions you must ask to gain clarity. If you're just getting started on your journey, and want to know what to prepare for and expect, then sections at the start of the book will provide the answers you need. Finally, if you want to set up some powerful daily routines, and learn to make use of the connection between your conscious and subconscious mind, then dip into the middle portion.

My advice, though, is to read it from cover to cover. Creating the life you want is a journey and there are different stages you must pass through. If you don't break through society's conditioning and learn why authority is not to be trusted, it can be hard to believe in yourself when you feel like a lone voice taking on the system. Furthermore, if you're not comfortable in your own skin, it can be challenging to promote yourself, or your work, to others and convince them to invest in what you're offering. Also, if you don't learn how to build a routine and structure your day, it can be difficult to create the habits needed to make an impact. Your journey will reveal all the lessons needed to advance and provide the emotional armour necessary to endure any attacks you'll face.

So, take flight. Let this book be your guide as you attempt (and then succeed) at living life on your terms. There are few greater rewards than being able to say you crafted your own existence. Today marks the first step of achieving this aim.

PART 1: BREAKING FREE

"What you know you can't explain, but you feel it. You've felt it your entire life, that there's something wrong with the world. You don't know what it is, but it's there, like a splinter in your mind, driving you mad."
- **Morpheus,** *The Matrix*

Must you accept the world as it is? Are you doomed to live out your existence conforming to a set of working, and social, norms that severely limit your freedom and creativity?

Many people think they are. They believe in the might of the system and think there's little they can do to escape its way of life. So, they carry on; attempting to conform, accepting, medicating and ignoring the nagging of their inner voice.

But what if you were to start asking questions or to rebel? What would happen? Would you be ridiculed, silenced or attacked? Or, would you be praised, followed and loved? You'll never know until you have the courage to make the leap.

Breaking free can mean many things. It might be quitting your job. It could be rejecting your religion. Perhaps it means leaving a relationship. While all of these steps can be important (although are, by no means, a necessity), there's one aspect of breaking free that every person seeking to create the life they want must embrace.

Every person desiring to break free from a life that imposes limits on their opportunities and enjoyment must free their mind. They can no longer think like everybody else.

Your outlook must change. Your belief system must alter. Your self-talk must be radically different. This is the first step and true definition of what it means to break free. The day you disconnect from the mass mindset, is the day anything, and perhaps everything, becomes possible for your life.

To get to this moment, and have the confidence to make the leap, you'll need a new perspective. You need to understand why trusting authority can be dangerous. If you find that a 9 to 5 lifestyle is leaving you drained, you need to realise that there are alternatives. Furthermore, if you've always been someone whose kept their true personality and opinion hidden behind the veil of societal acceptability, you need to learn about the power of embracing your individuality.

Learn this knowledge, take these steps, and you'll not only be happier and more comfortable in your own skin, you'll become more powerful. The limits that prevent others from taking action will no longer apply to you. You'll discover that the system's boundaries can be pushed further than most people think. And, once outside these boundaries, you'll develop abilities and skills you never imagined yourself capable of possessing.

Of course, it's understandable that you might be slightly reticent when it comes to breaking free. You've probably got people around you who warn you of the consequences of separating yourself from the tried and trusted path through life. Furthermore, it can be scary when you're trying something new.

If this is the case, then try to shift your nerves to excitement. Alongside risk, you'll find opportunity. Yes, you're taking the metaphorical stabilisers off your bike, but this could be the moment that you fly.

For the moment, prepare your mind by reading the following four chapters. You'll discover life guidance that you have unlikely ever heard from your parents and teachers. You'll find out why many of our powerful institutions are not to be trusted. Finally, if you've ever felt that you're not normal, you'll learn how this experience can be used to your advantage.

So, get ready to break free. Life will never be the same again.

CHAPTER 1: GUIDANCE FOR LIVING AN EXTRAORDINARY LIFE

Who can you turn to for life guidance? If you're lucky, maybe you had enlightened parents who nourished your talents, encouraged your dreams and taught you that anything is possible.

Or, maybe you had no guidance at all. Beyond being told to study hard at school, get into university, find a well-paid job and get married and have kids, your parents never mentioned anything else. They certainly never told you to listen to your inner voice or do what you feel is right.

Where does this leave you? Perhaps you're uncertain about who to believe. On the one hand, the system is offering you a life of boredom and unfulfilled potential yet seems to be the tried and trusted path that most people take. On the other, this book appears to be offering you the freedom and fun you crave but could be leading you down a path fraught with danger.

You have a difficult choice to make. Do you choose certainty and accept that life can never be the way you want? Or, do you embrace the unknown, risk losing it all (supposedly), but give yourself a shot at greatness?

Before making your choice, perhaps you'll want to weigh up your options. What does each path entail? The great news is that you can learn from other people's experiences. You aren't the first person to have made this difficult decision. Many have stuck with the system's path and it's useful to learn from them as their life draws to a close.

When choosing a path, it's important to realise that society won't provide you with any guidance on how to live an extraordinary life. It will only give you a narrow selection, from a limited menu, and tell you to be happy with what you get.

Is that good enough for you? If not, read on to discover a unique form of life guidance that will help you in your decision to break free.

Why you should aim for the "impossible"

If you've ever felt like you don't belong, or that the options the system presents for making a living are barely worth living for, then I'm going to present you with a solution. It's not your fate to spend your life compromising your dreams, values, opinions, free time, friendships, loves and morals. You *can* have everything you want but, in order to create a life where you do, there's a mindset shift you must embrace.

In the film, *The Gambler*, Mark Wahlberg plays University professor Jim Bennet, a compulsive gambler whose losses have put him in the hands of the local mob. His flaws are many. Besides the gambling, he also leaches off his rich mother and has a hand in fixing college basketball games.

One thing he doesn't do, though, is pretend to himself. He's honest about who he is and what he wants. In a monologue, delivered as his world crumbles around him, he tells his girlfriend,

> The only thing worth doing is the impossible. Everything else is grey. You're born . . . as a man . . . with the nerves of a soldier, the apprehension of an angel, to lift a phrase, but there is no use for it. Here? Where's the use for it? You're set up to be a philosopher or a king or Shakespeare, and this is all they give you? This? Twenty odd years in school which is all instruction on how to be ordinary . . . or they'll fucking kill you, and they fucking will, and then it's a career, which is not the same thing as existence . . . I want unlimited things. I want everything. A real love. A real house. A real thing to do . . . every day. I'd rather die if I don't get it.

Are you brave enough to admit you want the same? Most people aren't. They've been conditioned by society to believe that "wanting everything" is selfish. As a result, they deny their desires. However, by doing so, their lives become more about fulfilling society's, and other people's, expectations than honouring their inner voice.

What does Jim mean when he tells us that, *"The only thing worth doing is the impossible?"* That the life you truly want, the one your soul is crying out for, is seen as impossible to achieve by the system we live in.

Think about what you're conditioned to believe from a very early age. You're taught that you can't be happy all the time. You're taught that dreams don't come true. You're taught that you can't have everything you want and that, inevitably, you must compromise on almost everything. This is what Jim means when he talks about, *"instructions on being ordinary."* Therefore, the only thing worth doing is defying these instructions and following your soul on the journey it's urging you to take.

This is the change you must embrace. You must accept and acknowledge that your soul wants something greater than what society offers.

It's unlikely you'll achieve the impossible without some form of criticism. People will say you're crazy and selfish. Don't listen to them. Instead, realise that an urge to challenge society's "instructions on being ordinary" is what causes every social and technological advance.

- Was Nelson Mandela wrong for challenging a government that wanted to suppress its people's freedoms?
- Was Roger Bannister wrong for challenging the idea that running under 4 minutes for a mile physically impossible?
- Is Elon Musk wrong for challenging the fossil fuel industry by insisting electric cars are the future?

Of course not. Therefore, you shouldn't feel wrong, or be deterred, from wanting, and aiming at something fantastic for your life.

So, embrace your desires. Never play small. Admit what you want and put everything you have into achieving it.

How to avoid living a life you regret

In 2009, Bronnie Ware wrote a blog post about her experiences as a palliative nurse. She worked caring for patients during the last twelve weeks of their lives and made note of their most common regrets.

This blog post went viral, gaining over a million views in a year and landing her a book deal. Her book, *The Top 5 Regrets of the Dying*, sells well to this day. We'll now explore these five regrets and look at solutions to avoid missing out on what's important in life.

Regret Number 1: I wish I'd had the courage to live a life true to myself, not the life others expected of me[2]

Throughout our lives, we have two voices vying for our attention. The first, is our inner voice. This speaks to us through the language of dreams, desires and deep emotions. It urges us to pursue the people and activities we feel most passionate about or fascinated by.

The second, is society's voice. This speaks to us through the language of expectations and commonly held beliefs. It urges us to conform.

Typically, the second voice is stronger and more prevalent than the first. However, if you don't want to end up living a life of regret, then you must learn to silence it.

What is your heart telling you to do? Leave your job? Or, start working on your dream so you can work towards leaving your job?

Perhaps it's telling you to leave a relationship? Or, maybe, you need to pursue a relationship that, up until now, you haven't had the courage to go for. Whatever the case, start making decisions based on what your heart is telling you. Amazing things happen when you do.

Nelson Mandela was born into the Thembu tribe (in the Eastern Cape of South Africa) in 1918. Although considered a third-class citizen in his country, within his tribe, he was in a relatively privileged position. Taken under the wing of the King, he had his education paid for and was set for a life of being a royal advisor.

However, as Nelson was exposed to the wider world, and became of aware of the horrendous injustices that were occurring in his country, he could no longer ignore the call of his inner voice.

His heart told him to fight apartheid. During a 50-year struggle, he sacrificed his freedom, time spent with his family and a relatively wealthy and harm free life as a royal advisor, to pursue what he believed was right. Ultimately, he played a major role in liberating a nation because he resisted the expectations of his tribe and royal guardian.

Of course, taking such a bold step is not without consequence. However, whenever you feel the pressure of your parents, friends and bosses causing you to question your decision, just remember they don't have to deal with the fallout of regret. You do.

You are the one who is going to wake up 30 years from now and have to explain to yourself why you chose to ignore your inner voice. They either won't be around or will have completely forgotten the hassle they gave you. You can't escape yourself.

Regret Number 2: I wish I hadn't worked so hard[2]

Why are you working so hard? Beyond the understandable need to put food on the table, why are you giving so much to a job that would replace you within a week?

Is it a misguided sense of loyalty? Is it societal conditioning, making you think you're lazy if you don't work beyond your contracted hours? Why do you do it?

If the reason is anything other than necessity, or because you love your work, then start cutting back.

- Refuse to regularly work beyond your contracted hours.

- Consider finding a job where you only work 30 hours a week.
- Work as a freelancer so you can be in charge of your time.
- Use the Gig economy to mix and match jobs so you have more free time.

You may think these suggestions are naive, and that financial and work practise necessities won't allow for such freedom, but what choice have you got? Would you rather end up on your death bed, regretting spending 40 to 50 hours a week of pretty much your entire adult life being somewhere you didn't want to be, doing things you didn't want to do?

Regret Number 3: I wish I'd had the courage to express my feelings[2]

Don't keep it locked inside. Whether it's at work, in a relationship or creatively, you must express yourself. This might mean telling your team you have an idea for a new product or that you think a campaign should go in a new direction. It might mean telling your boss you're not happy about a situation.

In a relationship, it might mean expressing your love for another person without fear they'll reject you. Or, it could mean expressing something you're not happy about without fear of offending them.

There might be things you want to say and create. Maybe you have a message to share with the world but are afraid how people will react to it. Perhaps there's a product you want to build, or a picture you want to paint, but are concerned it might fail. Whatever the case, and in whatever the situation, do not fear the consequences.

Far worse than ridicule or rejection, is the possibility of illness or loss of spirit. Bronnie mentions that, "Many developed illnesses relating to the bitterness and resentment they carried." It seems you are faced with a choice. Either release your emotions or let them consumer you. It's no secret that cortisol, the stress hormone, has been linked with a multitude of illnesses and conditions from hyperglycaemia to suppressed thyroid function and high blood pressure.

On top of that, it's harder for people to develop strong emotions for you, and what you do, if you rarely express yourself. Sure, other people might leave you alone and think you're "ok," but do you really want to breeze through life unbothered and unnoticed? If not, you must express what you feel inside. You might draw criticism for your outspoken ways but, after a while, people who feel the same as you will be drawn to your cause.

Muhammad Ali is a great example of the transition that can take place when you have the courage to be yourself? Initially, he was despised for his seemingly radical stance on joining the Nation of Islam, changing his name and refusing to fight in the Vietnam War. However, despite this condemnation, these were causes he felt strongly about and, therefore, saw no reason to hide his beliefs from the world.

With the passing of time, public perception towards Ali changed. People began to respect the bravery it took to stand up for what he believed in and were drawn to his charismatic personality (another example of how powerful expressing yourself can be). It wasn't long before the hatred turned to love and Ali became one of the most admired figures of the 21st Century.

Regret Number 4: I wish I had stayed in touch with my friends[2]

Why do we lose touch with our friends? To answer that question, we must look at where most people spend their time and what they prioritise.

The average working week in the UK is 42 hours and 18 minutes.[3] That's not all, though, as you can expect an average commute of nearly an hour a day. Then, when you're not working or commuting and if you're married and have children, it's likely you're spending time with your family. On the face of it, this is something you want to do. However, the question remains, when do you get time for yourself or to maintain old friendships?

Where we once lived in tribes, villages or communities, the system we live in is driving us into ever smaller units. We have our husband or wife, our one to three children and that's it. The old saying, "it takes a village to raise a child" no longer applies. Time spent apart from the family is viewed as selfish and, as a result, we must give up our friends and pastimes.

To find a solution to this regret, you must fight society's conditioning and rethink current ways of working and living. Perhaps working longer, in attempt to get wealthier, isn't the answer. Maybe spending more time with your family, in an attempt to appear selfless, isn't either.

What would happen if you worked less and focused more on your quality of life? And, would your relationships actually improve if you spent *less time* with your significant other and more time engaged in soul enriching activities like seeing friends, travelling and hobbies?

You have a choice. If you want to create a new societal norm then you must take a stand. The status quo is maintained because of apathy and acquiescence. Start saying, "no" and it gives others permission to do the same.

Regret Number 5: I wish I had let myself be happier[2]

Avoid an "I'll be happy when . . ." mentality. Some people won't allow themselves to be happy because they haven't got a job. For others, it's because they're not in a relationship or don't have children. Some are perfectionists and find it hard to be happy unless everything is the way they want.

Whenever you lose sight of the fact that happiness is a choice, remind yourself of this Tyler Durden quote, "This is the greatest moment of your life and you're off somewhere missing it."

All you have is now! This moment. That's it. If you can't be happy with it, then what makes you think, two or three years down the line when you achieve the goal you imagine your happiness to be dependent upon, you will be then? You won't. You'll just be looking for a new goal to achieve or, circumstance you imagine is blocking your happiness, to be removed.

Break out of this cycle. You don't want to look back on your life and realise there was nothing preventing you from being happy. Think of all the great times you'll have missed out on and all the extra energy you could have lived with but didn't, because you put conditions on your happiness.

So, allow yourself to be happy right now. You may feel your hang ups, or personal issues, prevent you from making this transition but these too, are largely illusory and either future focused or past generated.

The only thing real is now – what you're doing and how you're feeling in this very moment. Don't carry anything with you that can prevent you from experiencing the happiness you deserve.

You might find the top 5 regrets of the dying surprising. They appear to be encouraging you to create the life you want and warning you against following the crowd.

This is not how most people live. In fact, most people live as if there isn't even a choice. They select one of the limited options that society presents them with, work hard and keep their heads down. There's little consideration of the idea they might be able to choose, or even create, the life they want. And yet, once they reach the end of their lives, they wish they'd explored the deeper promptings of their soul.

Are you going to wait that long? Don't be fooled into thinking you are without a choice. Remember, reaching the end of your life and regretting your decisions is not an outcome you are doomed to experience. You can change your path today.

What happens if you don't follow your dreams?

Look at the graph below. The vertical axis is a difficulty rating. On the horizontal axis, is a timeline, starting at 25 and continuing until 75. The line which starts at 4/10 represents the path of a person who, aged 25, is faced with a life changing opportunity but decides to stick with the path they know (the easy path). The line which starts at 9/10 represents that same person's progress through life having decided to take this opportunity and pursue their dreams.

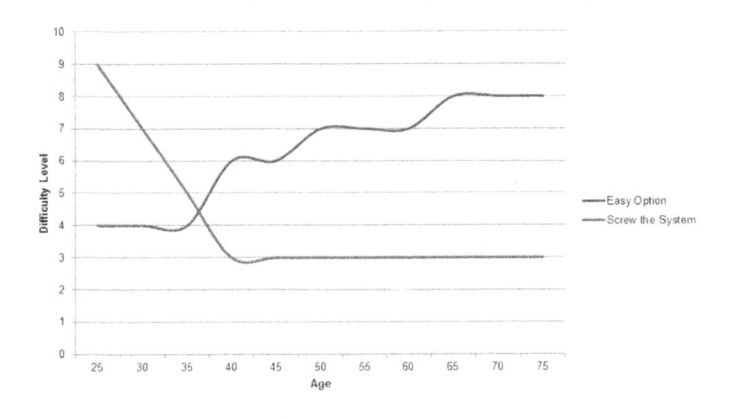

Before any analysis can begin, it must be noted that 25 is a generalised age. Your life changing opportunity may come earlier or later. However, when it does, the questions, fears and possibilities that we'll now explore will all arise. Which path will you choose?

Upon discovering your dream, it's usual that a flood of positive emotions will encourage you to explore further. However, as the euphoria dies, and you're faced with the reality of making some important changes, a new feeling emerges.

Fear enters your mind. What if I fail? Will I go broke? What will other people think? All of the outcomes you're taught to avoid are brought to the forefront of your mind when you attempt to break free and pursue a new life. As a result, you might do a quick mental check, comparing the two paths and evaluating what each one entails.

When doing this, the classic mistake is to focus short term. Yes, the initial stages of pursuing your dream are far harder than sticking with what you know. Expect to be short on money. Don't be surprised when your decision is questioned by colleagues, peers and loved ones. Brace yourself for initial failures.

This is why living your dreams starts at a difficulty level of 9. It will test you to the limit. However, note that it is *not* a 10. No matter how hard times get, they will not break you, so long as you believe in the ideal that prompted you to make the initial decision.

The other option is continuing to walk the easy path and remaining at a difficulty level of 4. You've got a job; you're paid enough to live comfortably and your future seems secure. Furthermore, the next 10 years (if you're around the allotted age of 25) will play out in a very similar fashion. Marriage and children are on the horizon, as well as a house of your own and a good disposable income. Sure, you'll have to work hard and manage a lot of stress but it's more than likely you'll avoid any significant life challenges.

Even before 40, though, the two paths will merge. Research suggests that it takes 10 years or 10,000 hours to become a master at any given field. This means that by 35, the person who decided to pursue their dreams is beginning to reap the rewards of their decision. Perhaps their new business has experienced a few years of profit, or their books are selling thousands of copies a month. As a result, their life is getting easier. Not only are they beginning to be rewarded materially, they are experiencing true success. The feeling of joy that accompanies beating all the odds washes away the memories of the initial hardships.

The reverse could be said of the person who has stuck with the easy path. For them, cracks are starting to appear. Maybe it's at 40, 45 or even 55, but there comes a point in most people's lives when they question its meaning. If the answer is little more than making money, doing enough to survive or what has been expected of me, then expect a loss of vitality. This is why the difficulty level rises for the easy path. You may still have your job, marriage, house and a good income but, the slow decay of your spirit will take its toll.

For many, old age is something to be feared. A loss of health and ability can lead to a sharply decreasing quality of life. However, for the person who follows their dreams, age can have a surprisingly minimal effect - If your mind stays young, then your body has no choice but to follow.

The same can't be said of the person who follows the easy path. What, at first, appeared to be the hassle-free option now presents you with a mountain of difficulties. There's an ever-increasing chance that, at sixty-five or even seventy, you still have to work to put food on the table. However, you are no longer a youthful twenty-five-year-old.

Forty years of working at a job that offers nothing more than financial reward has taken its toll on your health and energy. As a result, life is hard. Not only do you have to contend with physical deterioration, you must also carry the burden of unfulfilled potential.

Of course, this is a generalised analysis. You may discover your dream earlier or not until a mid-life crisis sparks a dramatic change. You may be relatively happy with your life, even without a passion to follow. However, if you hear the calling to pursue something greater yet are having doubts about taking the leap, then remember this one thing – *hiding from who you really are, and what you're really here to do, won't remain easy forever*!

CHAPTER 2: FREE YOUR MIND SO YOU CAN ACHIEVE THE IMPOSSIBLE

English libertarian, John Stuart Mill, noted in his book, *On Liberty*, that current opinion is almost always flawed. He pointed to Jesus and Socrates, declaring them two of history's greatest figures and remarked that, in their day, they were criticised and persecuted.

This, he claims, is a trend that continues throughout the ages. The "bad guys" of today are the heroes of tomorrow (the change in public opinion regarding Muhammad Ali, Gandhi and Nelson Mandela provide more modern-day examples and lend further credibility to this hypothesis). What does this change in perception tell you?

The words I want to ring in your ears as you read this chapter are, "current opinion is almost always flawed." Whatever the mainstream media, government, your religious leaders and teachers are telling you, is most probably detrimental to your life. You must scrutinise their advice and assess whether there is an agenda behind their instructions.

Almost always, there is, and because history has not been kind to conventional opinion, you must seek to detach yourself from the majority. The periphery is where you'll find your answers. Make this space your home and you'll begin to excel because the limitations that apply to most people won't restrain your efforts.

So, get prepared for a trip down the rabbit hole. Like Neo in *The Matrix*, you've taken the red pill. It's now time to discover how the institutions that bring order and guidance to the masses, are actually holding you back.

Why you should stop living in the "real world"

When I was at University, I frequently heard people talking about the "real world." Typically, a tutor, someone with a job, or my parents would warn me about what was waiting once I left the bubble of higher education. They'd make comments about being "out in the real world," as if the life I'd been living up until that point had been a dream. Apparently, there were some inescapable truths I wasn't going to like.

To start with, I was going to have to work 40 to 50 hours a week for the next 40 plus years of my life. Furthermore, there was a good chance I wouldn't enjoy this work because most people didn't (according to a Right Management survey only 19% of employed people in the US and Canada reported being "satisfied" with their work).[4]

I had to accept this condition of economic servitude, though, because there were things like mortgages, rent and pensions that needed to be paid for. It was a scramble to win the rat race and, as a result, most of the people in my life were to become like commodities – either there to be manipulated to my advantage or used to prevent loneliness and the social humiliation of being a loner.

In this largely meaningless existence, the aim of the game was making money to either survive or thrive. There was the dual motivation of avoiding going broke and aspiring to a lavish lifestyle that was supposed to make me happy. I'd reach the pinnacle if I was able to buy a large home, expensive cars and afford a few vacations a year. All of this would occur while supporting a family I was going to be too stressed out to appreciate. Free time would be non-existent. If I wasn't working, I'd have to be taking care of my family responsibilities.

This was the "real world." I was about to enter a reality where dreams of a happy, exciting and meaningful life were just fantasies. Life was going to be a long list of written and unwritten rules that I had to follow and expectations that had to be met.

Was I scared of entering this realm? Yes and no. While I would have chosen death over this soul-sapping half-life, I didn't believe I was compelled to conform. Three years prior, I'd watched a movie that had a profound impact on my consciousness. Exiting the cinema, after having seen *The Matrix*, I was left with a feeling there was *something wrong with reality*.

In *The Matrix,* Neo is plugged into a network that feeds him a computer-generated version of reality. This world is dull, routine, grey and almost lifeless. However, because he has never experienced anything else, he believes it to be real.

This perception changes, though, when Neo is contacted by a freedom fighter called Morpheus. He unplugs Neo from *The Matrix* and shows him that another world exists. In this new reality, Neo's possibilities, and capabilities, are far greater than he ever imagined. He learns Kung Fu in a matter of moments, can leap from building to building and discovers that the only limit on what he can achieve is his own belief.

The Matrix is very similar in nature to our concept of the "real world." Both have their rules and regulations, programmes and modes of operating. Furthermore, both are accepted as the truth about the way the world works. In fact, it's this assumption of truth that makes these "realities" so dangerous.

When you believe the "real world" represents the truth about life, you never bother to explore what lies beyond its confines. Think about all the innovations, and advances in the cause of humanity, that wouldn't have occurred had people like Einstein, Galileo, Gandhi and Mandela just accepted the, "that's just the way the world is" line.

Most people won't look in the places they're told there's nothing to find. That's why it's so dangerous to accept the "real world." You could be missing out on innovation, adventure and freedom because you don't believe it exists.

The Matrix gives you an insight into our "real world." It also provides a glimpse of what happens when you "unplug." Far from facilitating the disaster your parents, teachers and peers predict, it opens the gateway to super human abilities and an extraordinary life. This can be seen with,

- Galileo discovering evidence to support the theory that the earth rotated around the sun. This turned the Christian world's geocentric paradigm on its head and was achieved because he refused to believe what the church told him.
- Nelson Mandela, and his comrades, relentlessly campaigning for justice. This eventually emancipated a nation and overthrew an entire political regime. Such

- an incredible feat was achieved because Mandela refused to that a governments power was absolute.
- Bruce Lee transcending physical and racial boundaries with his martial arts. This enabled him to become an inspiration to millions and was achieved because he refused to believe that his heritage would hold him back.
- Emiline Pankhurst helping bring the vote to 50% of the UK population (back in 1919). This empowered millions of people and was achieved because she refused to believe that women weren't capable of understanding political issues.

These outstanding achievers had one thing in common - they didn't live in the "real world." In their realities, notions of whether something was acceptable, or possible, didn't exist. As a result, there was nothing to clip their wings and prevent them from realising their unique destinies.

Could the same apply to you? What could you achieve if you refused to accept the outlooks, attitudes and beliefs that hold so many people back?

Why trusting authority can be dangerous

We're conditioned to respect authority. From an early age, we're taught to listen and obey. Whether it's our teachers, the police or bosses, the assumption is that they know what they're doing and are acting for the greater good.

Is this assumption correct, though, and what happens when you look deeper into the institutions that rule over us and scrutinise their motives and behaviour?

Take the police or judicial system, for example. While on the surface, they may appear to be protecting citizens and maintaining order, an alternative theory can also be offered. Are they, in fact, maintaining the present power structure and ensuring that the status quo is upheld?

The shambolic history of the war on drugs seems to indicate this is the case. A series of policies, first enacted by Nixon in the 1970s, has led to a situation where police officers are financially incentivised to make soft drug arrests. As a result, non-violent offenders are clogging up U.S jails at ever increasing rates. Some, fuelled by hysteria whipped up by the media, receive outrageous mandatory minimum sentences. These have the terrible consequences of depriving hundreds of thousands of people of their liberty, enraging communities and creating an underclass more likely to engage in crime now that a criminal record severely restricts their employment opportunities.

Police standards have also declined as a result of these policies. Mediocrity is being incentivised and, as a result, less time is given to serious crimes like rape and murder. It's all about the numbers. If an officer can fulfil quotas with soft drug arrests, then why spend the weeks and months necessary on more serious cases?

The politicians and corporations don't care though. The former can swagger around pretending to the electorate that they're tough on crime and the latter get to profit from a source of cheap labour.

The police and the justice system aren't the only institutions whose authority needs to be questioned. Scientists and researchers have become Gods in the western world. Their discoveries, and even theories, are blindly accepted as the "truth" by an awe struck public.

Ironically, this was not always the case. The scientific community was, at first, the anti-system voice. With their evidence-based discoveries, they slowly liberated the masses from the religious paradigm and all of the limiting beliefs that went with it. However, times have changed, and since the scientific community has become part of the establishment, it too has been infected by the system.

An example of this can be seen with corporations paying scientists for a stamp of approval on their products. One particular case, in 2015, saw a group of scientists claim there was little link between obesity and drinking sugary soft drinks like Coca Cola.

After making these outrageous claims, it was then discovered that these scientists, working at institutions including The European Hydration Institute, The University of Hull, The National Obesity Forum and The British Dietetic Association, had all received funding from the Coca Cola corporation. Their "research," which runs counter to claims made by the British Journal of Sports Medicine, indicated that there was little link between diet and obesity and that factors like physical activity played a more important role in maintaining health.[5]

This kind of manipulation is far from being an isolated incident. There have been similar cases with the tobacco and alcohol industries and, most damaging of all, the persistent denial of man-made climate change that is perpetrated by some scientists.

Regardless of the case, the pattern is always the same. A corporation with zero ethics pays a scientific institute to carry out "research" whose subsequent findings benefit their agenda. The reason a corporation does this is to gain the scientific seal of approval. As mentioned early, a lot of people revere scientists as modern-day Gods. What they say *has* to be true and, therefore, their product must be great if a scientist says so. However, what this sorry state of affairs reveals is that the scientific community is run by people, not Gods, and, in some cases, the pursuit of the dollar has become more important than the pursuit of the truth.

Governments shouldn't be trusted either. In the 2003 Iraq War, the US and UK governments lied to their respective populations when they claimed that Saddam Hussein's regime was in possession of Weapons of Mass Destruction and posed a threat to the western world. However, subsequent investigations revealed that there were no WMD's and the UN condemned the US and UK for acting against its charter by invading Iraq.

Such actions run counter to what we're taught to believe about our governments. They're supposed to be full of intelligent people who know what's best for their citizens. Of course, they have to make tough decisions, with severe consequences, but they always act for the greater good.

Or do they? As more travesties like the one above come to light, it's becoming widely understood that governments act in the interests of a tiny elite. This elite fund their campaigns, assisting a political party in being voted into office and forming a government. When this happens, elections promises are often ignored as the government pays its debt by passing through laws that bring greater profits to their backers, or turning a blind eye to their unethical behaviour.

Of course, governments hide this agenda through a litany of advisers and PR. They'll tell us it's for our own protection when they're caught spying on their own citizens and the extent of their surveillance operation is revealed. They'll tell us we need to fight for our freedom when invading foreign countries that pose no direct threat to our populations. They lie to us again and again. So why should we believe them?

I've included these examples because I want you to realise that you have no moral obligation to play by the system's rules. In fact, you don't have to be, or do, anything other than what you want. Don't let a false sense of duty influence you to fight for a country that doesn't care. Think twice about applying for a job you have no passion for but your parents think would be a good career. Regardless of your teachers and careers advisers' protestations, don't go to university if you've got a passion elsewhere that you're keen to explore.

Happiness and fulfilment are found through rejecting authority. They're experienced when free from obligations, duties and the notion of what you *should* be doing with your life. You're taught to play it safe, get a well-paid job, don't cause any trouble, work hard, follow the crowd and respect authority. However, nine times out of ten, this is going to lead to a boring, meaningless life where the only rewards up for grabs are security and comfort.

If that's something you don't want then you must start *rejecting* almost everything authority figures have to say. They *are not* trying to help you. They are trying to control you, or manipulate you into buying their products.

Trusting authority will limit your life. You, and you alone, are best positioned to decide what to do with your future. Of course, you may want to seek advice from others and this can be useful. However, when people or institutions start *telling you what to do*, understand that those instructions come with an agenda.

The examples presented, showing the fallibility of the police, scientists and government, are designed to make you realise there is no power greater (at least not man made) than yourself. When faced with the might of the system, it can be easy to think that the individual is irrelevant and that you have little choice but to conform. But why conform to institutions that lack the correct moral foundation? And why conform to parents whose wishes are driven by a fear of what might go wrong?

There's no good reason to do so. Sure, there will be *pressure* to obey authority but, if your actions and decisions aren't breaking the law, this is all you'll face. Isn't the chance of a self-determined life full of meaningful achievements, and experiences, worth a bit of ridicule, criticism and condemnation?

Why you must protect your mind against the media

In 2015, I visited my Grandma for her 99th birthday. It was just after the terrorist bombings in Paris. Over a cup of tea, we discussed the events and I was shocked by her thoughts.

She was genuinely concerned, even fearful about the prospect of more ISIS sponsored terrorist attacks. I agreed that it was concerning but then remembered she'd lived through World War Two. So, I asked her, "But surely Grandma, this is nothing compared to the war?" To my astonishment, she replied that she felt more scared now than she ever did during that conflict.

"How is that possible?" I asked her. In World War Two, millions of people died, Britain was being bombed on a daily basis and there was an imminent threat of Nazi invasion. However, despite these terrifying circumstances, my Grandma said that while living on a farm, in the north of Yorkshire, all the events of World War Two never seemed *real* to her.

I left the conversation perplexed. As tragic as it was, how could 130 people being murdered in Paris compare to the horror of the World War Two?

And then the answer hit me. Today's mass media didn't exist in the 1940s. There weren't 24-hour news channels filling people's minds with fear and 15 different newspapers reporting on the horror of the events in tiny detail.

This conversation with my Grandma was a lesson for me on the power of the media. Its influence is incredibly far reaching. If it can make the loss of 130 lives seem more terrifying than the loss of millions, then what else can it exaggerate to manipulate your mind?

Part of the media's ability to influence our thinking comes from the perceived authority it possesses. Journalists are believed to be educated and intelligent people on the hunt for the truth. They've been to university and got degrees. They've secured jobs at prestigious companies with imposing and trustworthy names like *The Times*, *CNN*, *Fox News*, *BBC* and *The New York Times*. Surely, they must know what they're talking about and wouldn't knowingly lie to us?

While I don't question the intelligence of reporters and journalists, I do question their intentions. Perhaps there was a time when the media was on a hunt for the truth and held major institutions accountable. After all, many organisations start with the correct moral foundation only to be corrupted as they acquire a measure of power. However, now, rather than shining a light on what's happening in the world, agenda promoting is what drives the media.

What is the bias of their readership or viewership? Which political party would it benefit the owners, and board, to have in power? Will sensational headlines or one-sided stories, that only bear a semblance to the truth, sell more than an article that explores an issue from all angles? This is the approach of the mainstream media and, as a result, the public get fed an incomplete, or distorted, picture of world events.

Behind this deception lies a cynical aim. The media want to make you believe you're in danger (see the prominence, and detailed coverage, that terrorist attacks and Covid-19 receive) or that a certain person, or group of people, is the enemy and poses a threat to your comfortable life. If they can manipulate you into believing this then there's more chance of you acting, purchasing and voting in a way that benefits their owners.

This is why you should be sceptical about anything you read in a paper or watch on the news. Perhaps the best strategy is to disengage completely. Don't watch the news, never buy a paper and scroll past sensational headlines on internet news sites. If you want to know what's going on in the world then seek out independent and credible sources to keep you informed. You won't get left behind and your world won't collapse. In fact, you might start seeing some positive changes.

For one, the likelihood of being triggered by partisan headlines, and stories, will be greatly reduced. Reacting strongly to an issue like immigration robs you of your energy. You might spend hours feeling outraged, preventing you from giving your dream the mental attention it needs to be brought to reality.

Another benefit of disengaging from the media is that you get to retreat from the "real world." Much of your ability to create a reality of your choosing rests on becoming a limitless thinker. If you're constantly viewing negative images of the world, and hearing about all the wrong doing, then you'll begin to think that a fun filled life, where you get to do what you love, isn't possible. You'll confuse the distorted image of reality that the media presents for an accurate depiction of how the world works.

In summary, the media's world can't help but drain you. It'll make you live in fear, potentially instil hatred in your heart, influence you to feel you're not good enough and, worst of all, limit your outlook. So, if you do watch or read anything presented by these sources then do so in the knowledge that they're promoting an agenda. The world might not be as terrible as it seems. There might be hidden opportunities that you're not being made aware of. As a result, the best strategy is to question everything and find your own answers.

How you are being manipulated by science

The system conditions us into believing we have little control over our lives. The outcomes we achieve, and our position in life, is all down to luck, random events, the talents we're born with or our genes. Never us. Never are we told in school, or by our parents, or in the media, that the individual plays the main role in determining whether they get to live a happy and successful life.

Even when it comes to our health, there's a consensus that it's largely out of our hands. "It's all about having healthy genes," doctors and scientists tell us. If you've got them, great. If you don't, well then you just have to accept your fate. However, as with most things, when you dig deeper into the system's conditioning, you find flaws in its dogma.

Below, is a section from *The Biology of Belief,* written by Dr Bruce Lipton. It reveals that, in two of the main life-threatening diseases people experience, genes play very little role in determining our health,

> In fact, only 5% of cancer and cardiovascular patients can attribute their disease directly to hereditary. (Willett 2002; Silverman 2004) While the media made a big hoopla over the discovery of the BRCA1 and BRCA2 breast cancer genes, they failed to emphasize that 95 percent of breast cancers are not due to inherited genes. The malignancies in a significant number of cancer patients are derived from environmentally induced epigenetic alterations and not defective genes. (Kling 2003; Jones 2001; Seppa 2000; Baylin 1997)[6]

Despite this evidence, what's the main message you hear about your health? It's, largely, out of your control. Yes, you can exercise, improve your diet, stop bad habits like smoking, but, despite all these steps, you might still suffer from some type of cancer or another horrible disease.

Modern medicine has taught us this. Through its myopic focus on the importance of genes, it has conditioned us to give up responsibility for our physical well-being. We're victims, in need of intervention or help, rather than sovereigns, powerful and in control of our own health.

You might have believed that your genes play the dominant role in your health had you not read Dr Lipton's counter claims.

Now, having heard both points of view, you are faced with a dilemma. Which information do you trust?

Both are supported by scientists. However, one is backed by the recognised scientific paradigm of the day and the other is a relatively obscure study that only a few people are aware of.

Herein lies a problem with modern science. It defends the dominant paradigm and suppresses anything that challenges its hegemony. In his book, *The Structure of Scientific Revolutions*, physicist and philosopher, Thomas Kuhn, discusses this behaviour. He writes,

> Normal science is based on the assumption that the scientific community knows what the world is like. Furthermore, much of the success of the enterprise derives from the community's willingness to defend that assumption, if necessary, at a considerable cost. Normal science tends to suppress anomalous facts because they are a roadblock in a pre-committed theoretical path.[7]

The dominant scientific paradigm of our day is that genes play the determining factor in our health. This even extends to areas like addiction or laziness. In illnesses that should be entirely preventable, like heart disease and lung cancer (when caused by smoking), we're now having our power removed to an even greater extent because we're being told there might be an addictive or lazy gene.[8]

Is this the truth? Absolutely not. However, it is the dominant scientific paradigm.

Thomas Kuhn suggests that paradigms will be defended at a "considerable cost." The scientific community has a lot riding on its knowledge. Now viewed as the keepers of the truth, their position as a modern-day God's rests on the general public's belief that they know how illness works. Therefore, if some evidence, or a study, was to occur that challenged one of their paradigms, it is more than likely to be discredited or ignored. As Kuhn states, anomalous facts will be suppressed.

What does this mean for you? While it would be foolish to deny the overwhelmingly positive role that science has played in liberating mankind from superstition and dogma, it shouldn't be beyond scrutiny. Challenge scientific paradigms. Listen to voices on the periphery of mainstream science. (In his book, *The Science Delusion*, Dr Rupert Sheldrake highlights that even the speed of light isn't constant). Look for the information you're not taught at school or university.

If "normal science" is now in the business of defending its status and power, it can't always be relied upon to challenge the status quo in a way that reveals new, liberating insights. Furthermore, if it suggests you should believe information that harms or disempowers you, then know you're within your rights to challenge its claims.

Remember that the scientific community is made up of people and people are fallible. They *will* promote a course of treatment that's harmful to you if it's supported by their industry and puts money in their pockets. Therefore, you must be brave enough to push back against their opinions when they threaten your autonomy or well-being. Perhaps you don't need anti-depressants or any form of medications. You might be better off reading books or even visiting a therapist or healer. Don't be afraid to act and make decisions outside the dominant paradigm.

Why you can push the system's boundaries far more than you think

The system wants you to believe that life is full of boundaries. First, we have our laws, banning certain types of behaviour and punishing those that partake in them. Then, we have our unwritten rules. Depending on the country, society or culture you live in, there are things you aren't supposed to do. Perhaps it's marrying outside your race or religion or perhaps it's focusing on your passion, rather than your education, and refusing to go to university. Whatever the case, certain decisions and behaviour will be deeply frowned upon, and even punished, by your friends and family.

On top of these, there's another layer of boundaries that suppress our behaviour and dreams. Science is often telling us about our limits. These can take the form of physical or mental limits, like the aging process or a low IQ. Or, they can take the form of universal limits, like having a finite amount of time and operating in the hard, clunky world of matter.

As a result of spending our lives being told there's so much we *can't do*, our maps of the world shrink. We operate in tiny realities where we work jobs that are boring yet comfortable, and have lifestyles that are repetitive yet safe.

This is an unconscious trade. We give up the greater prizes of adventure and freedom because we believe we live in a world full of boundaries and limitation. Instead, we accept the next best thing - security and comfort – and cling onto these with a fear we might descend into a life of struggle and hardship.

But are these boundaries real and what happens when you test them? Could you be denying yourself the opportunity of a greater life because you've never stopped to question the stories you've been told? The following example might make you think twice.

Frank Lucas was an American criminal who operated from the 1950s to the 1980s (his life was portrayed by Denzel Washington in the 2007 film, *American Gangster*). Towards the end of the 60s and start of the 70s, he became the country's number one heroin importer. He did this by cutting out the middle man and travelling to Vietnam to set up a trafficking route that involved local producers and the US troops fighting in the war. The troops would smuggle the drugs back to the US in hidden compartments underneath the coffins of their fallen comrades. Once the heroin was on the street, Lucas estimated that he was making close to a million dollars a week.

As incredible as this was, though, it was perhaps even more amazing that he didn't face any serious prosecution until 1975. This meant that, for over 25 years, he got away with committing criminal acts every single day of his life. Even when the law did catch up with him, he maintained some level of control. Despite being incarcerated, he ran a drugs empire from his cell and had steak and oysters smuggled in so he didn't have to eat prison food.

A story like this defies euphemisms like "crime doesn't pay" and "nobody escapes the long arm of the law." Lucas did. For almost three decades, he broke the law with impunity and faced no serious consequences. Where was the system's power? It was both ineffective and insufficient to trap Lucas's guile and intelligence.

You would be wrong to read this and think that I'm promoting a criminal lifestyle. I believe in creation and bringing love into the world, not destruction and causing pain. However, I'm still fascinated by Lucas's story because it exposes the façade of the system's power.

If Lucas could order people's deaths, rob at will and then flood a city with the most reviled drug known to man, for nearly three decades, then the system is not as powerful as it would have you believe. Perhaps its control over your life is maintained by the fear of what it might do, rather than what it actually can do. What if all the things you've been told are impossible, or frowned upon by society, or "not how the world works," are just as malleable as the laws that failed to apprehend Frank Lucas?

Before I add to this point, it must be explained that I'm not advising you to break the law. Doing so won't bring you the happiness and fulfilment you desire. However, you will have to test the system's boundaries and break through the unwritten rules of society.

When you do, you'll discover that most of the boundaries are illusions. Adopt Frank Lucas's mind-set, if not his methodology. When talking about what brought him success in the world of crime, he had this to say,

> The main thing that popped into my head was that I had to be willing to go hard. I needed to not play it safe. I'd gotten to this point by taking huge risks. Nothing ventured, nothing gained. Going out to Asia had been a huge undertaking, something people just didn't do. And I'd had no fear whatsoever that I could make it happen. I needed to remember that the next time a possibility that seemed crazy presented itself to me.[9]

Taking risks and breaking boundaries go hand in hand. Other people will tell you what you want isn't possible, and warn you of the consequences of failure, but this is the risk you'll have to take. Find out for yourself what lies beyond the system's boundaries. Perhaps it's the rewards reserved only for the brave.

CHAPTER 3: CHALLENGE THE 9 TO 5 TO FIND SOMETHING GREATER

What is a 9 to 5? Ostensibly, it's the number of hours most people are required to work for their employer. Of course, there are variations, depending on the country you live in and their employment laws, but these figures tend to represent the minimum number of hours you'll be working each day.

Perhaps you work more. A 9 to 5 rarely means working between the hours of 9am and 5pm. It's more likely to mean 9 till 6, 8 till 6, or, in extreme cases, 7 till 7.

Then there's the commute. If you haven't got the money, or don't want, to live in the vicinity of the place you work, then it's likely you'll have to make anything from an hour to a three-hour round trip each day. You're then looking at the possibility of 75 hours of your week being taken up by your job.

It's not just the hours, though, that are so oppressive. What you're required to do within them can be just harmful to your soul as being overworked is to your health. Work a 9 to 5 and it's likely you'll be,

- Forcing yourself into a role, and set of behaviours, that are out of harmony with who you are.
- Working for nothing greater than financial return.

- Compromising your values, ideas and opinions for the sake of "playing the game."
- Indirectly (and sometimes directly), involved in committing unethical acts that harm other people and the environment.

Who wants to live like this? Very few people it appears (statistics from a 2017 Gallup survey reveal that only 15% of the world's workforce are engaged by their jobs).[10] Make no mistake, this lifestyle is lived out of obligation rather than choice.

I'm urging you to reject the 9 to 5 and everything that goes with it. Consider your deeper motives for working. Pursue a method of making money that uplifts, rather than drains you. Here are a few criteria to guide you on this journey,

- Inspiration, rather than fear or perceived necessity, guides your decisions.
- Success is measured by how good you feel rather than the money you make.
- Joy is gained by giving to other people rather than using them as a means to your advance.

Understandably, the prospect of making such a radical change might be scary. It may seem you're purchasing a one-way ticket to a life of poverty and unemployment. Sure, it sounds like a great way to live but, surely, the demands of living in the 'real world' would prevent your life from ever being this way.

I disagree. Following your inspiration *can* work. There's a common misconception that many people have when it comes to making a living. They believe they can only make money through *what* they do (e.g., I build houses, I manage accounts, I

SICILY
2025

SOPHIE & HARRY

SIRACUSA

23-30 June 2025

FLIGHT: U2 2845
BRS TO CTA
SORTED! HAPPY CHRISTMAS X

@ ST JAMES PARK

THURS 12.06.2025
MILLBURN STAND @ 16.00

YOU'RE GOING!

MERRY CHRISTMAS!

People Watching
SAM FENDER

arrange schedules). What they don't realise is that people get paid, or get paid the most, for *why* they do something (e.g., I create homes, I give people financial freedom, I help people perform at their best).

Simon Sinek discusses this in his brilliant, *Start with Why*, Ted talk. He asks you to consider the technology giant Apple. Customers are happy to not only purchase computers from them but also phones and tablets. This is because they stand for something. They believe in challenging the status quo and thinking differently. It's not just about what they do – making user friendly computers – it's about the why behind everything they do – to put empowering technology in the hands of millions.

People who believe in these values will then buy Apple's products. As Sinek explains, this happens because customers, clients and employees make decisions based on the limbic/feeling part of their brain. Whether you directly communicate your purpose verbally, or whether it's communicated through everything you do, other people will be *moved* to buy from, and work with you, if you're following your inspiration.

These are the dynamics behind the exchange of money for products and services. It's why you can follow your inspiration and still make a very good living. As a result, you don't need to work a 9 to 5 and the people that tell you otherwise are, probably, too afraid to try. Why continue listening to them when you can prove to yourself that something greater is within your grasp?

Why it's bad to have a "good job"

"How's John doing?'"
"He's doing well. He's got a good job working in the city.'"

The above dialogue is representative of many conversations I had during my 20s. They typically took place when meeting old classmates and parents of friends.

Upon hearing the reference to a good job, I used to just nod my head and issue a standard response. Something like, "Oh that's good to hear," or, "Great news! Where are they working?" However, after a while, I started to question what this term meant.

A "good job" usually refers to employment in banking, finance, law, accountancy or a similar profession. On paper, these are dream jobs. If you were to secure such a position, your parents would be proud of you and your friends would be jealous. However, what is the reality of these occupations?

Dig a little deeper into the "good job" myth and you'll find cracks in the perfect picture the term presents. These cracks run along two fault lines that we'll now explore.

The first is a lack of satisfaction. This can be caused by uninspiring work, excessive working hours and submission to corporate culture. What's good about working 50 plus hours a week, feeling stressed and tired all the time? What's good about having to "play the game" and silence your ideas and opinions on how things should be done? And what's good about performing the same role, day in, day out, year after year working for a company that has no greater goal than to make money?

While research indicates that satisfaction levels are higher amongst "good jobs" than in manual low skilled employment, they also show that the greatest satisfaction is found by those who work a job they are good at, or that directly improves another person's life. This is where a "good job" fails. The typical "good job" completely ignores the need to feel that you're working towards a cause greater than yourself. In a "good job," the cause is profit. While such a motive may breed compliance, it won't bring a sense of fulfilment.

The second problem with a "good job" is the questionable ethics. More often than not, your actions will indirectly, or unintentionally, harm someone else or the environment. This is because the system we operate in is built on competition rather than cooperation. It teaches us to pursue profits regardless of the costs. Shareholders need to see a return on their investment and, if this means damaging the planet, or ruthlessly taking over another company and destroying what it stood for, then so be it.

Examples of a lack of regard for ethics are abound. In 2013, Barclays were fined $443 million for manipulating energy prices. Individual traders, targeting markets on the west coast of America, deliberately caused losses in one part of the electrical market so they could adjust prices of the financial contracts they owned. These contracts were linked to the price of electricity (which they'd just manipulated) and, as a result, netted them $35 million in profit. However, by doing this, they caused losses of well over $100 million for other investors and pension funds.

In a series of emails that were used in the case against Barclays, individual traders were recorded boasting about what they were doing. One stated that he was going to "crap on" certain markets and another replied that he, "loved it" and was going to have "fun" with the index they were manipulating.[11]

While we might read these comments in a newspaper and find them offensive, we still praise friends and family members who work in these industries. We deceive ourselves by saying they're isolated incidents, failing to see the rotting core at the heart of the "good job."

Look a little deeper, though, and it's there for anyone to see. Lawyers who defend the guilty or knowingly prosecute the innocent (see Prosecutor Elizabeth Lederer and the Central Park 5 case), treating justice as a game and seeking loopholes in the law. Accountants who do everything they can to ensure corporations pay as little tax as possible, leaving the taxpayer to pick up the revenue shortfall. The financial sector, with companies like JP Morgan, Goldman Sachs and Citigroup, through sheer greed and blind pursuit of profit, all playing a role in the global financial collapse of 2008. The list goes on. Endless amounts of people work in companies whose doctrine of "profit above all else" reaps untold misery for millions of people all over the planet.

So, what do I now say when someone reels off the, "So and so's doing well, they have a good job in the city'" line? My response is this, "No, what you mean is they have a well-paid job."

There's a huge distinction between a good job and a well-paid job and it's important to realise the two terms aren't synonymous. A good job may, or may not, make you wealthy but it will inspire you, encourage expression and creativity, treat you with respect and understand that there are other areas of your life just as important as your work. A well-paid job will reward you financially but it could well steal your time, vitality and even your soul.

How to recognize the signs you need to quit your job

It's always been thought that being employed, even if it was just for the sake of it, was better than being unemployed. The theory is that you'll have something to do and boosted self-esteem through being financially independent. If you're unemployed, you'll lack direction and be more likely to slip into debt or fall victim to a litany of vices.

Times have changed. It now seems that the lack of meaning, humiliation and frenetic pace that go hand in hand with modern jobs is more damaging to your mental health than being unemployed. Working a job you enjoy is still the ideal scenario, but a 2011 study, conducted at The Australian National University and reported in BMJ Journals, revealed that the psycho-social impact of working a job you dislike is worse than being unemployed.[12] Such evidence begs an important question – is it time for you to quit your job?

Understandably, the thought of doing so might be scary. There are clear risks to quitting your job, especially if you don't have a new one to move into and you've left without a plan or strategy for what you'll do next. However, at what point does taking this risk become necessary to preserve your dignity, health and enjoyment of life? And, are these qualities more important than financial reward?

We'll now explore the 10 signs you should quit, or be working towards quitting, your job. As you go through them, try to assess the severity of your situation. Are you just angry because you've been overworked for the last couple of weeks and, when the workload dies down, you'll be happier? Or, is the unhappiness permanently there, regardless of differing circumstances?

After answering these questions, perhaps you'll decide to hold out a little longer while you explore new options. Or, perhaps you should have left years ago and this reminder will give you the impetus to take the leap. Whatever the case, it's important to realise you are not chained to your job and there are *always* other options available. So, without further ado, here are the 10 signs you should quit your job.

The first warning sign is feeling low on a Monday and high on a Friday. Just because almost everybody else you know feels the same, don't make the mistake of thinking it's normal to live this way. It's not. You shouldn't be dreading the onset of the working week and celebrating the end of it. This is your life. You can't spend it wishing you were somewhere else.

The second warning sign is clock watching throughout the day. Of course, keeping track of time is not an issue. However, frequently looking at your watch is a clear sign of a lack of stimulation.

Work doesn't have to be this way. It's possible for you to be so engaged by the tasks you undertake that you lose track of time. That's the kind of job you should be looking for. If your current role doesn't provide this stimulation, you should consider other options.

The third warning is sign is that you can't wait to leave at the end of the working day. If, at 5.30pm, you're logging off and running for the door, it's a sure sign you're working purely for the money. If you enjoy your work then you don't mind carrying on for an extra half hour to ensure your customers or clients are satisfied and you do a great job.

While the previous three signs are a warning, alerting you to the idea that you're not stimulated by what you do, the next two are of more serious concern. If either of them applies, then you should be thinking of quitting your job sooner rather than later.

The fourth sign is damage to your health. Perhaps you're being exposed to dangerous chemicals or a hazardous working environment. More than likely, you're under so much pressure, and having to work so many hours, that your stress levels are dangerously high. You might also be permanently exhausted through lack of sleep, unhealthily overweight through lack of time to exercise or relying on excessive drug use (both legal and illegal) to keep you going or because it's part of the work culture.

If this is the case, then there's something you must understand. *No amount of money can make up for permanently damaged health.* Get out soon or, even better, play the system and get (paid) time off for stress while you look for other work.

The fifth sign is not being treated with respect. A 2013 study, by online career site Glassdoor, revealed that appreciation is one of the biggest motivators in the workplace. 80% of employees say they are motivated to work harder when their work receives recognition.[13]

We all want to be treated fairly and with respect. Therefore, if the goalposts are being moved when it comes to being paid a bonus, you're being lumbered with an extra role but not getting a pay rise, you're being spoken to in a dismissive manner and regularly given tasks at 5.25 pm, which need to be ready for 9 am the next day, then you must stand up for yourself. Explain that you won't tolerate this treatment. If it continues, hand in your notice.

Continual compromise of your values, and sense of justice, is detrimental to your character. It erodes self-respect. Long term, this is more important than money.

The next three signs will let you know if you're ready for the transition. They give you an idea of what you should be working towards. Meet these criteria, and you'll have a stable platform to aim at a more exciting future.

The sixth sign you're ready to quit your job is that you've built up a healthy side income. This might be through a new business you've created or a new skill you've acquired (e.g., becoming a personal trainer and seeing clients outside your regular working hours). Once you're earning the *minimum* amount of money to survive on, through this venture, my advice is to quit your regular job.

Take the word minimum literally. Your side income doesn't need to be earning you enough to afford vacations, cars and meals out. It just needs to cover your overheads and put food on the table.

Why is this the right time to quit? Because freedom is more valuable than money. It doesn't matter if, initially, you can't afford the lifestyle of your friends. By quitting just as soon as you have enough money to cover your living expenses, you're buying an abundance of time for your passion. This will make you richer in experiences, well-being and, long-term, possibly even wealth.

The seventh sign is having enough money saved up to live a year or more without working. If used productively, a lot can be accomplished in a year. Even without any plan for what you will do, taking a year out and learning more about your passions and interests might still be worthwhile. And, if you're certain about your passion, and have even started making money on the side, then a year could be all you need to turn it into a full time living.

What's the worst that can happen? Even if you didn't make any headway, it's more than likely, at the end of the year, you can find another job similar to the one you had before.

Furthermore, there's a chance you *will* be successful. You have no idea what you can achieve with a fully committed year. Remove the exhaustion of a job you dislike and the time constraints of working 40 plus hours a week, commuting and other commitments, and you'll be a different person. This new lease of life could lead to a massive increase in productivity. Furthermore, with the peace of mind that comes with not thinking about money for at least a year, you're free to give it your best shot.

Only you will know the exact amount of money you need to save to make this work. Make sure it's enough to cover all your living expenses with, perhaps, some extra to get your new business or project running. Certainly, it doesn't need to be so much that you're taking vacations every quarter and spending without restraint. Remember, the focus of this year is creating a new life, not seeking temporary pleasures that need to be paid for by unfulfilling work.

The eight sign is that you've set a "quit date" and it's fast approaching. A "quit date" is a designated date you've set for when you'll leave your job. It's a good idea if you've been meaning to leave for a while but keep baulking when it comes to taking action.

When you set a "quit date," mentally, you've already made the decision. You know it's the right thing to do. Perhaps you have some money saved up or are earning through a side income. Maybe the situation at your job has become so untenable that you must leave regardless. Whatever the case, your mind is made up. However, as the date approaches, you're starting to have doubts.

If this is the case then you must remember what you're experiencing is normal. You're about to take a risk and risks can make us feel uneasy. Your need for certainty will be challenged. However, if you've been planning this for months (or even a year), you must see it through.

You've set your "quit date" for a reason. Whether it was to move towards a new life, or escape a toxic environment, your decision wasn't made in haste.

With fear removed, you decided that it was time for a change. With fear present, you might be wavering. However, you must remember fear often impairs your ability to make good choices.

Therefore, you must stick with your "quit date." Your better judgment led to this moment so see it through.

The final two signs you need to quit your job can be classified as exceptional circumstances. They're intuition-based decisions. A clearly constructed plan of action might be irrelevant if you gut is telling you to quit. Sometimes, you just have to jump and deal with the consequences.

The ninth sign is that you have a "calling" which you've been ignoring for years. A calling is a deep, nagging intuition that there's something you need to do, or a place you need to be. Often, this urge will reveal a path that is uncertain and risky. In some cases, it might not lead to a clearly defined career or money-making opportunity.

This was the case for Saroo Brierley. In the film *Lion*, based on his life story, Saroo was separated from his mother and brother at five years old. Taken to a local orphanage, he was then adopted by an Australian family with whom he spent the rest of his youth and adolescence.

While at university in Australia, he gets the urge to reunite with his original family. Unable to silence these thoughts, he spends more and more of his free time investigating the location of the orphanage where he was adopted and the train station where he last saw his brother. Eventually, he even travels back to India in a seemingly futile attempt to find two people in a population of billions. He has a faint memory of his mother and brother and longs to see them again, wondering what's happened to them and whether they're still alive.

Saroo gave up a lot to pursue his calling. As a result of all the research he undertakes, he becomes distant from his girlfriend and neglects his studies. However, despite the negative impact this has on his life, he feels compelled to continue.

Ultimately, he's successful. Using Google Maps to retrace his steps, he finally reunites with his mother. The intuition that drove him to travel half-way across the world and take a million to one shot at locating someone with no idea what city they lived in, was correct.

If you've experienced a "gut pull" similar to Saroo's then you'd do well to follow his example. Explore your calling. It might lead nowhere. It might lead to the life of your dreams. You just can't tell until you start acting on the promptings of your inner voice. Even if there's no immediate avenue to make money, one might present itself as a result of your journey (this was the case with Saroo, who turned his story into a book and then sold the rights to make a film).

One thing is certain, though, if you stay in your job and ignore your calling, you might be dealing with a mountain of regret in your latter years. Far better you find out now.

The tenth sign is that you're totally dissatisfied with your life. Perhaps you've experienced a crisis and you're starting to question everything. You realize your time on this planet is finite and don't want to waste another moment. Furthermore, you know you're falling short on realising your potential and hate to see it waste away at a mundane job you don't enjoy.

Blogger, Jon Morrow, experienced this in 2006. A car crash that left him incapacitated and with multiple broken bones, made him question his entire life. He wasn't happy with what this introspection revealed. Coming to the conclusion that he'd been neglecting his dreams, he decided to quit his job and attempt to make a living through blogging.

With an abundance of time to dedicate to his new craft, it only took Morrow 5 months to make money online.[14] Ten years later, he was one of the kings of the blogging world, owning Smartblogger and holding a position as associate editor with Copyblogger.

This would be impressive for anyone to achieve. The fact that Morrow made this brave leap, and scaled these heights, while suffering with SMA (Spinal muscular atrophy, a disease that destroys motor neurons in the brain and prevents the sufferer from speaking, walking, breathing and swallowing), makes his example all the more impactful. The lesson is clear.

Hitting rock bottom, and having nowhere else to go, can be the perfect time to change.

What lesson can you take from his story? Your rock bottom might not have anything to do with your financial situation. Instead, it might be the end of a relationship or struggling with addiction. Whatever the case, the feeling of dissatisfaction is strong. For the sake of your self-respect, you know you must change. If this means quitting your job then so be it. Even though the odds might be against you, sometimes desperate situations facilitate miracles. It will certainly focus your mind and make sure you're being productive.

With these factors on your side, dissatisfaction can be a great reason to change. Seize the moment this feeling creates and start building your new life right away.

Is your work a "life mission" or just a job?

"Do you want to sell sugared water for the rest of your life? Or, do you want to come with me and change the world?"

- Steve Jobs

This is the line Steve Jobs used to lure then President of PepsiCo, John Sculley, to work with him at Apple. It worked. In an interview for *Bloombery Game Changers,* Sculley recalls the impact this appeal to the "bigger picture" had on his decision.

He left behind what many would consider a fantastic job. President of one of the world's most recognisable brands, his marketing campaigns, in the late 70s and early 80s, had been instrumental in stealing market share from Coca Cola. He had vast wealth, control over his working life and the satisfaction of knowing his contribution was having a direct impact on the company's success.

So, why change? Why take the risk of leaping into the unknown when you're already onto a good thing?

In answering this question, we must engage in a deeper analysis of Jobs' appeal to Sculley. Sure, by society's definition, Sculley was fantastically successful but what was he really doing?

Selling sugar water. Jobs was right. Sculley had a product to sell. Nothing more. No matter how a marketing team might have tried to spin it, selling cans of Pepsi was *not* changing the world. However, what Steve Jobs was offering did.

Jobs wanted to create technological advancements that pushed the boundaries of personal computing and altered the way people worked, communicated and had fun. It was a *mission* and this was the key to its appeal.

The difference between a job and a mission is vast. At its core, a mission will always be driven by a desire to create change. When following your mission, work doesn't feel like work, the hours spent on the project are irrelevant and the satisfaction gained from success is vast.

Added to his, people benefit from the work you do. Look at Gandhi. His mission was to achieve Swaraj (independence from British rule). By working towards this goal, he helped increase economic self-reliance, build bonds between Hindus and Muslims and provide inspiration for civil rights movements around the world.

Bruce Lee is another example of how impactful having a mission can be. His was to become the first oriental film star to rival the big Hollywood names. In doing so, he brought entertainment to the homes of millions, inspired many to learn martial arts and challenged stereotypes about Asians.

People with missions advance the cause of humanity. Whether it's by fighting oppression, creating scientific or technological breakthroughs or simply inspiring others with their amazing skills, they create change. Their reward for doing so is a meaningful life.

Contrast this with having a job, and it becomes clear why Sculley left PepsiCo. A job tends to be self-serving. You're out to make yourself money. Financial reward, security and status are part of the motives. Fear also plays a role. Whereas people with missions are driven by a *love* of what they do, or a burning desire to right a wrong, a fear of poverty and social exclusion are some of the motivating factors that drive people to seek jobs.

A job rarely benefits anyone (apart from those at the top of the company making all the money). Take Pepsi for example. Job's description was right. At best, people working for Pepsi could claim they're supplying the world with a tasty drink. At worst, and probably more accurately, they're destroying health and contributing to an obesity problem.

This analysis may appear extreme. However, the lack of employee satisfaction in modern jobs demonstrates that something is missing. Could it be your need to make a difference and have a positive impact on other people and the world?

Talk of missions and changing the world may seem daunting. I hope that by using the examples of Steve Jobs, Gandhi and Bruce Lee, I'm not scaring you into believing you could never find your own. A mission can exist in any line of work. You find it when your motivation for working is deeper than money. Whether this means discovering that within your present job, or moving to a new field, the option to create a meaning for your work is always there. What do you want to change?

CHAPTER 4: EMBRACE YOUR INDIVIDUALITY AND SHINE

*"The reasonable man adapts himself to the world.
The unreasonable one persists in trying to
adapt the world to himself.
Therefore all progress depends on the
unreasonable man."*
- **George Bernard Shaw**

Would you consider yourself an unreasonable person? What would your friends, family and colleagues say?

Surely, you'd want them to answer with a resounding "no." Afterall, reasonable is good. Reasonable is likeable and easy to get along with. You're never going to get any trouble from reasonable. However, reasonable people just accept things the way they are.

Have you ever noticed that, amongst all the people who change the world, or experience phenomenal success, there's a common factor? They don't think like everybody else! In fact, they're on a completely different plain of consciousness. Whereas most people look at the world and see an endless stream of rules, obligations and boundaries they must conform to, the unreasonable person sees a playground where they can do what they want.

It's this difference in outlook that separates the reasonable from the unreasonable person. A reasonable person adapts to life and works within the parameters given to them. The unreasonable person does no such thing. Instead of accepting, they question. This defiance gives them the opportunity to create the life they want.

Despite the criticism they face, the world needs its unreasonable people. Where would we be if Galileo accepted the churches opinion that the earth was the centre of the universe? Where would we be if the Wright brothers understood man's lack of wings to mean flight was impossible? Where would we be if Steve Jobs had accepted that computers should only be in the hands of powerful organisations?

Ignoring the pressure to be reasonable, and embracing your individuality, is what leads to all of the great breakthroughs and discoveries of mankind. It will also enable *you* to live your dreams.

To do this, though, there's a trap you must avoid. When you feel isolated, and that the world thinks differently to you, it can be easy to fall victim to the idea you're "less than" everybody else. Unchecked, this can lead to self-doubt and the rejection of the unique opinion, point of view or creation that will facilitate your success.

Of course, you don't want this to happen. Therefore, you must understand that wisdom in numbers does not exist. Conventional knowledge is often the most flawed. Just because your idea or opinion is unique, doesn't mean it lacks value.

The individual is often the facilitator of change for the masses. You may not realise it now, but your determination to be true to your desires, opinions and beliefs is what will transform you into an unreasonable maverick on the cutting edge of your field.

This chapter is about owning your individuality. Everything that makes you unique should be embraced. This will not only ensure you're at peace with yourself, it might even provide you with a strategy for success.

Therefore, if you can't find your place in this world then create your own. Keep being true to who you are and what you want to do. The world may call you unreasonable to begin with, but it will thank you in the end.

What to do if you don't feel "normal"

If you're currently living with the erroneous notion that you're not normal, there's something you need to know. You don't have to change to be accepted by the society you live in. Instead, you can thrive by creating your own reality. Before you can achieve this glorious liberation, though, there are two questions you need to ask.

First, you must look deeper into what not being normal means. Ask yourself whether the so-called normal people, the ones you think have it all figured out, are untouched by moments of doubt or confusion. Do they breeze through life without a care in the world? Or, is it possible, they have issues that not even their wives, husbands or closest loved ones know about?

If there's one thing being a hypnotherapist for 15 years has taught me, it's there's no such thing as normal. Although society appears to produce a cohesive population, largely thinking and acting the same, everybody is different. *Everybody* has their secrets and insecurities.

There's no shame in feeling separate from this supposed whole. A lot of people do. It reflects nothing of your value or whether you're a good person. All it means is that you don't fit in with the dominant culture into which you were born.

This isn't a bad thing. Although you may struggle coming to terms with being an outsider, there are benefits to this position. Mainly, it frees up your time to pursue your goals and dreams. George Washington once said, "It is better to be alone than in bad company."

Approach your loneliness from this perspective and suddenly you have a world of time to dedicate to something worthwhile. While other people are out conforming to socially accepted norms, that never truly make them happy, you have the opportunity to fill your life with the activities, interests and people, that inspire you.

The second question you need to ask is whether there's a deeper meaning behind your struggle to "fit in." Is there is a reason why you don't feel a part of society? Could it be you're here to change it?

Whether this involves facilitating change on a political sense, a technological one or even creatively, progress is usually sparked by people who think outside the confines of societal norms. Therefore, you understanding the world differently could be exactly what's needed to bring about the new discoveries that humanity relies upon to continue its advance.

This is why you should never force yourself to "fit in." You could be turning your back on a gift or perspective that leads to an extraordinary life. And, for what? Surface level acceptance amongst your peers? In the words of Ian Wallace, "Why are you trying so hard to fit in when you were born to stand out?"

Alan Turing struggled with the inner turmoil of feeling different while craving acceptance from others. A brilliant mathematician, code breaker and designer of the first computers, Turing was an exceptional man yet he was far from what society considered normal. He was homosexual (in a time when it was illegal to be so), a loner and didn't understand or care for the normal graces and etiquettes of society.

His story is brought to life by the 2014 film, *The Imitation Game*. This focuses on the work that Turing, and a team of code breakers, undertook during the Second World War, as they attempt to crack the Nazi's Enigma code. The Nazis used this code to encrypt the orders for their entire war effort and it's estimated that Turing's success resulted in the war being shortened by two years and the sparing of 14 million lives.

Despite this service to humanity, though, Turing was treated shamefully after the war. Never publicly acknowledged for his work, he was forced to undergo chemical castration after being found guilty of gross indecency (his homosexuality was discovered).

During his "treatment" we see Turing (brilliantly played by Benedict Cumberbatch) at his lowest ebb. He's paid a visit by his old code breaking friend Joan (played by Kiera Knightley) who attempts to raise the spirits of her distraught companion. He looks at her seemingly happy life, compares it to his lonely and tortured existence, and remarks that, "You got what you wanted, didn't you? Work, husband, normal life."

Her response is something I want you to keep etched in your mind. If you ever struggle with embracing your individuality and wish that you were normal, then you must remember these words,

> No one normal could have done that [referring to Turing's work]. Do you know, this morning, I was on a train that went through a city, that wouldn't exist if it wasn't for you? I bought a ticket from a man who would likely be dead if it wasn't for you. I read up on my work, a whole field of scientific enquiry, that only exists because of you.
>
> Now if you wish you could have been normal, I can promise you, I do not. The world is an infinitely better place precisely because you weren't.

Why you should feel happy about being depressed

"You might have a chemical imbalance. Perhaps you should see a doctor. They'll give you something for it."

These were the words of advice offered to me by my parents. Although spoken with loving intent, they represented a surface level understanding of a much deeper problem.

I was at university at the time, two years into a politics degree that was becoming increasingly meaningless by the day. Alongside not enjoying my studies, I was disillusioned with the drinking and partying culture that dominated the universities social scene. I didn't feel a part of anything. Furthermore, I was uncertain about the future.

As I looked beyond my degree; I could tell that ending three numb years at university wasn't going to be my salvation. Instead, I foresaw future difficulties as I entered the world of work. Once again, I was going to be faced with heavy pressure to conform to a way of life I despised. Endless working hours, meaningless work and hiding my true feelings and opinions were a lifestyle I wanted no part of.

Despite these concerns, and my parent's advice, I wasn't depressed. Instead, I was totally uninspired by my life and the options presented for my future. Sure, I exhibited a lot of the symptoms - lack of sleep, low on energy, disinterested in life - and a psychiatrist may well have classified me as being so, but I knew my problem wasn't a chemical imbalance. In fact, it had nothing to do with anything *physical*.

Before we go any further, I need to make it clear that I'm not denying the existence of depression. However, it's my belief, and that of psychotherapist and author James Davies (*Cracked: Why psychiatry is doing more harm than good*) that most of what psychiatrists diagnose as depression has nothing to do with a medical condition. As Davies writes,

> As people struggle to cope with emotions and problems - unemployment, divorce, bereavement, the insecurities of adolescents - that have no basis in any mental disorder, psychiatry wades in and seeks to "medicalise" the situation. New syndromes, not based on any scientific evidence, are invented. Patients are misled into believing they suffer a condition that only exists in textbooks.[15]

If you feel depressed, or think you might suffer from depression, it's important to realise that the conventional approach to tackling this issue may do more harm than good. What if, like me at university, the issue isn't physical? What if you're suffering from an entirely different condition that needs a unique form of treatment?

In the film, *Fight Club*, Tyler Durden is the leader of a group of disillusioned men. His philosophy centres around doing whatever it takes to feel alive, letting go of the need to control and rejecting consumerism. In his centrepiece speech, delivered in the cellar of a bar, he tells the other Fight Club members,

> We are the middle children of history. No purpose, no place.
> We have no great war, no great depression. Our great war
> is a spiritual war; our great depression is our lives.

This speech explains the cultural malaise of our times and could shed some light on your discontent. Our crisis is existential, not chemical. We're depressed because we lack purpose. Whereas previous generations had defining historical moments, presenting them with a call to action or test of character, we have nothing. The greatest threat we experience is fighting our way through the crowds that block our path to the train or underground station.

What happens to your mind when it has nothing to live for? It begins to shut down. With no outlet to focus its attention, and no mission to demand all of its resources, it becomes absorbed by lesser goals and concerns. What am I watching on Netflix tonight? Am I looking good in my latest Instagram post?

These are our modern concerns. Combine them with endless hours spent working jobs we don't enjoy, and the disconnecting emptiness of the isolated lives we live, and the picture gets clearer. Becoming depressed, in a society like this, *is normal*. In fact, it's a sign of your sanity.

With a greater understanding of your discontent, you may wonder what you can do to deal with your unwanted emotions. The first step, bizarrely, is to rejoice!

Congratulations, you're not a robot. There's nothing wrong with you for feeling frustrated, bored and depressed. In fact, your discontent could be the key to a much greater and richer life. It's a sign you weren't built for mediocrity and a reminder to set your sights higher than you currently do.

Start thinking about what you accept. Are there situations or relationships you dislike, yet tolerate, because you believe you can't do better? If so, change this thinking. There's always something greater for you to experience and achieve. Realise this, and start working towards a greater vision for your life.

Next, question whether you need medication. Society is going to put you under a lot of pressure if you feel depressed. While the worst thing you could do is refuse to talk, you must be cautious about who you tell. Quite often, parents, friends and doctors have all been programmed to accept the dominant scientific paradigm of the day. At present, this states that medication is the most effective form of treatment for people going through internal struggles.

Are you going to be strong enough to challenge that pressure? You could be presented with facts proving the mood raising effect of medication. Combined with authority figures advising you to take this path, it might appear an inescapable option. They'll say you're naïve. They'll tell you that they're experts and know what's best. As a result, you may begin doubting yourself. After all, you're just an individual up against the opinions of an entire system.

If you ever find yourself in this position, then consider the other side of the debate. Sure, some medication has been proved to raise your mood, but what about the side effects? Are you willing to trade the absence of low moods for the possibility of nausea, diarrhoea, headaches, insomnia and decreased sex drive? Furthermore, what about the difficulties associated with coming off medication and the prospect of, potentially, using it for the rest of your life?

For these reasons, you must think very carefully about using medication. Approach it as a last resort. In extreme cases, it might be useful, but how extreme is your situation? Is there really nothing that can be done?

What new books can you read? Are there any good therapists you can consult? What lifestyle changes – diet and exercise – can you make to naturally enhance your mood? Most importantly, will changing your outlook (realising you must aim for something greater than the life presented by the system) give you an understanding of your situation that enables you to live with renewed vigour?

All of these questions should be answered before you even consider medication. Your feelings exist for a reason. To have them medicated away masks the underlying problem.

Some of the most brilliant people have suffered with low moods. Take Winston Churchill for example. Throughout his writing, he references the "Black Dog" that came over him after particularly testing events. If he had lived in modern times, might he have been medicated? And, if he was, would this have numbed the effectiveness of his mind?

Churchill lived in a time before medication so we'll never know. However, perhaps the lows were part of his personality and what made him great. To remove these would have potentially stopped him caring as much and diminished his leadership qualities.

He, as you do too, need your feelings. They may drag you down but they also contain the keys to your brilliance.

Could it be that most cases of depression arise because people aren't living a life? The opportunities society presents us for making a living are *so* dull. What if you need something else? What if you need something bigger?

The moment I committed myself to the pursuit of an uplifting dream, my depression began to lift. Perhaps you need to find something similarly grand. It may be a goal or a cause, the specifics aren't important. What is, though, is that you look beyond the confines of what society considers a normal life. In this space, you'll find what your heart desires and the energy this provides will make those dark days a distant memory.

Why you should be proud to be in a minority of one

There may come a time when you find yourself in a minority of one. Whether this is at work, pursuing a cause that is politically unpopular or going against the wishes of your family, everyone could be positioned against you. Does this make you wrong?

Before answering this question, consider ways of life that were once deemed normal and acceptable, yet are now reviled. Take slavery, for example. At one point in time, it was deemed acceptable to keep, and trade, other humans as if they were property. Some took advantage of this practice to enrich themselves. Of course, most weren't wealthy enough to own slaves but did they speak out against this horrible institution?

In time, some did. However, at slaveries apex, how many dissenting voices were there?

Would it have been possible that a lone individual, at the family dinner table or in a public meeting, expressed their disgust at the institution and was heavily criticised for doing so? Perhaps not a single soul came to their assistance (even if they might have secretly believed in what they were saying) and supported their point of view. Was this an indicator that the individual was wrong?

Now, we'd say no. They would be declared a hero and lauded for having the bravery to speak up against something we find appalling. So, is being isolated in your opinion a sign that you're incorrect?

Clearly not. However, how many people do we still treat as pariahs because they express points of view or ideas that go against the mainstream?

It might be at work, where someone challenges corporate culture by refusing to work beyond their contracted hours. It could be in a relationship, where one partner declares that although they love the other, they want to be intimate with other people as well. Or, it could be based around religion, with a Muslim or Christian, in a predominantly Muslim or Christian country or family, rejecting their faith. (Or, in a recent example, it might be someone challenging the official media and government narrative on the coronavirus outbreak and asking questions about the severity of the virus).

Such individuals are made to feel wrong for their opinions and actions. They rock the boat and, even if some people secretly agree with them, they're generally viewed as an annoyance.

It's far easier to go with the flow. Ignore your conscience and protect yourself. Yes, you may, at times, find it hard to live with yourself but no one is going to challenge you. You'll be left alone.

Despite apathy presenting an easy way out, though, you must stand your ground. It's every person's responsibility, and challenge, to stand up to, and throw off, societal conditioning. You must choose your conscience over what society deems acceptable. If you feel something is wrong, or there's a correct path for you to walk, then you must say or walk it irrespective of whether it challenges the majority. This is how positive change occurs.

Perhaps, in their hearts, slave owners knew what they were doing was wrong. However, they suppressed their conscience, making the justification they'd go out business if they didn't keep slaves or that, if everybody they knew was doing it, then it couldn't be that bad.

But it was. It was terrible back then (and we see that now), and the things we do because society deems them acceptable (pressuring people to work ridiculous hours, destroying the planet so the 1% can remain super wealthy, the existence of nuclear weapons) are terrible now.

So, if you're one of the few who fights against immorality, regardless of the amount of people who criticise your stance, be proud of your work. You may be standing alone for a while, but this doesn't make you wrong. History will affirm the validity of your stance and you could be part of shaping the future.

PART 2: DISCOVERING YOUR GREATNESS

Popular anecdote states that the sculptor, Michelangelo, could look at a slab of rock and already see a beautiful statue lying within. Therefore, his job, as an artist, was to chip away at the rough edges and reveal what was already present.

You are about to undergo a similar process. It's likely that, since birth, you've been blessed with an array, or one particular, talent or skill that could help you create the life you want. However, as you've developed, layer upon layer of societal conditioning, and your own self-doubt, has been heaped upon you, burying the inherent greatness.

Hopefully, after having read part 1, you have made some progress in ridding your mind of this conditioning. This should leave you in a position where you are now ready to unleash your talents and skills.

The following information will assist you in this transformation. You'll learn about the power of your habitual thinking and the ability it has to shape your future. Then, you'll be instructed on some of the skills needed to succeed at any endeavour. After that, you'll discover which practices you need to build into a daily route to ensure optimal performance. Finally, you'll learn what it takes to overcome the inevitable obstacles you'll face.

While reading, remember Michelangelo's statue. Sometimes, it can be hard to believe you could do, or be, anything significant, or special, when your life has shown little indication that this is the case. Fortunately, you do not have to remain bound to your past. Trust that within you, there are untapped reserves of genius, determination and drive. Once these come to the fore, your life will rapidly change. So, get ready to discover your greatness and reveal the best version of yourself to the world.

CHAPTER 5: CHANGE YOUR THOUGHTS TO CHANGE YOUR LIFE

Back in 1903, James Allen's book *As A Man Thinketh* was released. The title is an abbreviation of a bible verse from *The Book of Proverbs*. In its entirety, it reads, "as a man thinketh in his heart, so he is."

To our modern world, this is a curious promise. 21st century life is about the material. We value what we can see, touch and, most of all, possess. This is real. The laws of nature, which we believe we've discovered, govern how our universe works. As a result, we live with the belief we have almost everything figured out.

Compared to these discoveries, what is a thought? The materialist would probably dismiss it as irrelevant mental chatter or understand it as a reaction to the events of the day. However, what if the relationship was reversed? Is it possible that the thoughts in your mind determine the circumstances and events of your life?

It's a dangerous idea. After all, if you follow this line of thinking then you become responsible for the events in your life. If you spend too much money and slip into debt then you only have yourself to blame. Likewise, if, after years of stress, poor diet and lack of exercise, you experience a heart attack or develop a terminal disease, then you must accept responsibility.

Although both of these examples appear to have a physical cause – too much spending and poor lifestyle choices – there is a deeper trigger point. The debt might occur after persistent thoughts of impressing people with your gadgets, cars or clothes. Likewise, the illness might occur as a result of focusing on money to the exclusion of your health (and all the hours you need to work to generate it).

How do you feel about this diagnosis? Are you angry or upset? Do you dislike the idea of being responsible for your misfortunes?

While responsibility can be a bitter pill to swallow, there is a silver lining to this way of thinking. Surely, if you create your reality through thought then, within your ability, is not just the potential to harm your life, but the possibility of setting yourself free. Persistent thoughts of success will lead to their material and spiritual realisation. Likewise, persistent thoughts of health and harmony will lead to an optimally functioning body.

Society never promotes this idea. We're taught that the individual is powerless. Not only are we subject to the laws of nature, but we are also governed by the rules of society. As a result, life is out of our control. Illness, breakdown of relationships, accidents and our successes and failures have little to do with what *we* did. Instead, we are granted the comfort of excuses. It was our genes, our personality, our mental disorder or bad luck that caused us to fail or suffer.

Which option do you prefer? Are you willing to shoulder responsibility in return for the opportunity to create the life you want? Or, would you rather allow external factors to govern the direction of your life while you remain blameless?

After reading this chapter, my hope is that you will choose the former. In doing so, there is an important point to remember.

The Bible states that, "as a man thinketh in his heart, so he is." On first reading, this may appear to be an oxymoron. After all, we don't think with our hearts. However, on deeper inspection, the Bible hasn't made a mistake.

Thinking with your head is something that, according to a 2005 National Science Foundation study, occurs 12,000 to 60,000 times a day.[16] Most of these thoughts are repetitive (95%) and have little to no (direct) impact on your life. We can all attest to the fact that merely thinking once about a million dollars or a brand-new Ferrari doesn't result in their manifestation. However, thinking with your heart is something entirely different and is far rarer.

Thinking with your heart occurs when your thought generates an emotional reaction. This might happen when you're thinking about an upcoming presentation and a wave of anxiety travels through your body. Alternatively, you might be thinking about achieving your goal and it generates a feeling of joy. This is thinking with your heart and it shapes your reality.

Understanding the distinction between these two types of thinking reveals the key to being a positive thinker. A common misconception is that positive thinking involves imagining yourself doing well. For example, throughout your day, you might deliberately visualise yourself meeting your future husband or wife or reaching your sales target.

The reverse applies with negative thinking. Throughout your day, you might repeatedly, although this time unintentionally, see yourself failing. However, what happens if these thoughts, whether positive or negative, fail to trigger an emotional response?

Not a lot. The thought, lacking emotion, won't penetrate your subconscious and form a belief. You may have visualised yourself doing well but there's little impact on your life.

To be a true positive thinker, you must be a positive feeler. Relax, choose one specific goal, or outcome that you know would make you happy, and, from time to time, focus on this. After a while, you'll build up a connection with this goal or outcome and will train your subconscious to respond with a positive feeling. When this occurs, changes happen. You'll raise your energy and this will have a dramatic impact on your work, creativity, relationships, sports and anything else that's important to you.

Remember, though, this discipline takes time. Imagine yourself doing well even if, at first, you feel no emotional reaction. Work on releasing the negatives as well. If you catch yourself dwelling on an unpleasant memory, or fear of an event in the future, remind yourself to let go.

With time, you'll be able to generate a positive emotional response. When this happens, you'll discover that your mind operates in a similar manner to a computer. It *has* to obey your instructions. Positive thoughts, backed by emotions, will bring you answers and encounters that will advance you in the direction of your dreams.

How to use the power of belief to achieve your goals

In, *Star Wars: The Empire Strikes Back,* Luke Skywalker seeks out Yoda to complete his Jedi training. He's already used the power of the force to destroy The Empire's Death Star, and now he's ready to become a Jedi master.

Luke assumes that Yoda will help him achieve this aim. His previous mentor, Obi Wan Kenobi, has urged Luke to find him and, having trained Jedi for over 800 years, Yoda appears to be the best teacher in the galaxy. However, as soon as his training begins, Luke starts to have doubts.

He wants to master the light sabre yet Yoda has him moving rocks. Luke thought becoming a Jedi was about learning the physical skills to be undefeatable in battle. Yoda teaches him that it's about mastering his mind.

This frustrates Luke. He has no time for what he views as games. His friends are in danger and he needs to improve his skills as quickly as possible so he can assist them. However, Yoda insists on taking it slow and, as a result, a breakdown in their training occurs.

Yoda then instructs Luke to raise his sunken spaceship from the swamp. Using the force, Luke attempts but is barely able to raise it a few inches. Yoda takes over and elevates the spaceship out of the swamp and onto the land. Luke looks on, astonished, and utters the words, "I don't believe it!" Regretfully, Yoda replies, "That is why you fail."

Luke is stunned by this event and, as a result, his mind is finally opened. He begins to realise that life isn't governed by the material but, instead, by an invisible force that permeates everything and everyone. This force, if used correctly, will grant him superhuman powers and give him insights that both protect him from harm and reveal a path to his destiny.

On the surface, *Star Wars* is nothing more than an enjoyable movie. The concept of "The Force" is an interesting philosophy but its real-world applicability is limited. While most people would share this point of view, it's interesting to note that the thinking of early 20th century quantum physicists lends credibility to the philosophical underpinning of *Star Wars*. Max Planck, Nobel Prize winner for physics in 1922, once said,

> All matter originates and exists only by virtue of a force which brings the particle of an atom to vibration and holds this most minute solar system of the atom together. We must assume behind this force the existence of a conscious and intelligent mind. This mind is the matrix of all matter.

And Niels Bohr, who shared the Nobel Prize with Planck, said,

> Everything that we call real is made of things that cannot be regarded as real. If quantum mechanics hasn't profoundly shocked you, you haven't understood it.

What are these physicists talking about? Essentially, that the reality we live in, contrary to popular belief, is shaped by the intangible rather than the material. It's as Yoda explains to Luke. Our bodies and the objects around us are just "crude matter." What is far more real, and influential, is the energy that surrounds and runs through us.

What are the implications of this discovery? To create the life you want, you have to become a master of your inner world. *If you can believe something will happen, no matter how impossible it might seem to other people, this will be enough to turn your dreams into reality.*

How then, do you develop a level of belief sufficient to change your life? By following a formula explained by Maxwell Maltz in his bestselling book, *Psychocybernetics*.

Maltz, by trade, was a plastic surgeon. He would operate on patients for both medical and cosmetic reasons. After many years in practise, he noticed a strange phenomenon. While some of his patients would be delighted with the changes rendered by the surgical procedure, others, despite having what they believed to be their disfigurement removed, still felt ugly.

This puzzled Maltz. The procedures were a success yet the patient felt no psychological benefit. How could this be? It was then he discovered the importance of self-image and the process by which it is developed.

He theorised that self-image, not reality, governs the way people feel about themselves. Therefore, if a person believes they are ugly, little can be done to change their perception. They may have the bump on their nose removed but, because they believe they're ugly, they'll soon fixate on another aspect of their appearance they find displeasing.

Understanding this caused Maltz to dig deeper. How were these beliefs formed? After further study, he determined that *authority, intensity* and *repetition* are the three main forces that shape a person's beliefs (and that these are usually created, although not exclusively, in childhood). In the section below, taken from the book, he explains the interplay between these forces and how a belief is formed (the italics are mine),

> What we hear from a source we accept as *authoritative* - such as the father we see as omnipotent, from whom we desperately seek acceptance as a child - is given far more weight than the same statements if heard from what is to us at the time a less credible source. What we see, hear and experience with *intensity* - such as a father yelling at us, in front of others, making us humiliated - has added weight. And what we hear *repetitively* from authoritative sources has even more weight. Years after this programming has ceased, it may still be governing all sorts of behaviour.[17]

In this example, Maltz is explaining how negative beliefs, and behaviour patterns, are formed. However, what if you were to redirect the formula to positively influence your life? How would you use authority, intensity and repetition to form beliefs enabling you to create the life you want?

The first, and most difficult, aspect of this formula is authority. This is taxing because you can't do it yourself.

Contrary to popular opinion, self-affirmation is not the most effective way to form new beliefs about yourself. Research undertaken by William Swann at The University of Texas-Austin discovered that our self-esteem is based on our assessment of how likeable and competent we are. Who do we look to when gauging these levels? Yep, you guessed it, other people (especially authority figures). Furthermore, research undertaken by Swann's colleague, Robert Josephs, discovered that if you have low self-esteem, it's hard to program your mind through positive affirmations because you'll tend not to believe them.[18]

This is why fulfilling the authority aspect of the belief formula can be difficult (when trying to do it on your own). As important as it is to engage in positive self-talk, to transform your levels of belief to the point where they have a significant impact, you'll need a respected authority figure in your life.

Such a figure could take one of many forms. It might be a coach, mentor or even a member of the public. How you approach them is up to you.

With the coach, you might offer to pay them for their services. If they take you on, it's likely they already have some level of belief in your potential and, as the relationship develops, their advice and the affirming of their belief in you, starts to transform your own levels of belief.

The mentor might be a combination of a coach and someone important in your life who has achieved the goal you desire. If the personal connection is strong, you may not even have to pay them. Any advice or help you receive might be less structured than a paid coaching session but, perhaps, more meaningful. Afterall, they're mentoring you because they know you on a personal level and already believe in you. Therefore, when they encourage, and display their belief in you, it will rapidly transform the way you see yourself.

If you can't afford to pay a coach or you don't know any mentors, you could use a member of the public. The first place to start would be asking friends for feedback. They can tell you what they think of your new product or service or give an honest assessment of the skill you're trying to develop. Of course, being your friends, there might be a part of your mind that thinks they're just being nice and, therefore, you don't fully believe in their opinion.

If this is the case, take an even great leap. Put your work out into the world and leave yourself open to feedback. This might be achieved through book reviews on Amazon, comments on a blog or YouTube channel, entering a competition and winning an award or feedback from customers and clients who have paid for your product or service. If positive, you will have *proof* that who you are, and what you have to offer, is worthwhile. The belief you'll then approach your next project, person or performance with, will ensure the work, or you, will be at an even higher quality, or level, than before.

I experienced the benefit of having an authority figure supercharge my belief when I first started writing. After reading his books, *50 Self-Help Classics* and *50 Success Classics*, I emailed best-selling author, Tom Butler-Bowdon, to ask if he would provide feedback on my book (at the time, it was called *How to Live Your Dreams*). To my delight, he responded and we set up a meeting in his adopted home town of Oxford (Tom's from Australia).

I was nervous leading up to the meeting. My fear was that Tom wouldn't like my work and that the project I'd pinned all of my dreams on would come to nothing.

These fears quickly dissolved, though, as Tom offered his feedback on the manuscript. He pointed to a few chapters; said they were good but read too much like many other self-help books. However, he then pointed to my chapter on breaking free from the system, declared that it was excellent and encouraged me to expand on these ideas.

As soon as he uttered the word "excellent," I felt a rush of energy go through my body. Something had changed. I'd spent the previous 5 years repeating affirmations, trying to convince myself that I could become a best-selling author yet that one sentence, 5 seconds worth of time, did more for my self-belief than anything I'd been able to do on my own.

After our first meeting, the coaching/mentoring relationship grew. Each couple of months, I would send Tom a new chapter and he would provide feedback. I paid for his help, but the price was fair (that's why I describe him as a coach/mentor) and the boost to my confidence was priceless. My mind-set changed. I was no longer this crazy kid, spending hours working away on something that was, perhaps, completely futile. Now, I was a potential best-selling author because I had a genuine best-selling author who believed in my work. This is the power of having a positive authority figure on your side.

The second part of the belief formula is intensity. Using my story as an example, you can see that, when Tom returned his verdict on my writing, it had a deep impact. The emotional reaction was powerful.

You must look for a similar level when developing your own beliefs. Of course, an authority figure is the best source for sparking this level of emotion. However, you must also do some work of your own.

Get yourself feeling passionate about who you want to be, or what you want to achieve. Try to identify the emotions you'd feel if all of your dreams were realised. Then, work on experiencing them as frequently as possible. *Live in the state of your realised desire.*

Furthermore, celebrate your successes. Whether you do this with other people, or just take a moment to inwardly recognise what you've achieved, allow the emotion to resonate in your soul. Each success is a stepping stone to your ultimate destination and, by basking in the achievement, you're acknowledging your ability.

The final part of the belief formula is repetition. Work (and think) on what you want to achieve, or become, every single day. Seek regular feedback from authority figures. Keep reminding yourself, with intensity, that you can achieve whatever it is you want. Try not to let your mind waiver for more than a few hours. Of course, there are times when you need to focus on the task at hand, and there are times when you need to relax but, at all other moments, turn your attention to what you want to become. A new belief will form.

We'll now take a look at the belief formula in action. Mike Tyson used it, or unknowingly had it used upon him, to be transformed from impoverished child with low self-esteem, to multimillionaire, heavyweight boxing champion.

In the 2008 film/documentary, *Tyson*, Mike Tyson talks about this process. He mentions how, as a child, he was incredibly unsure of himself. He'd been bullied by the local neighbourhood kids and ended in up in a juvenile detention centre after being caught committing a series of robberies. As a result, he believed he was nothing. Other kids teased him and he received little love at home.

Despite this, though, he had an amazing talent that had the potential to change his life. His boxing prowess was first discovered by a man called Bobby Stewart. He worked at the juvenile detention centre where Tyson was being housed and quickly recommended him to professional trainer Cus D'Amato.

Cus had trained world champions before and it didn't take him long to recognise that, with the right tutelage, Tyson could go all the way to the top. At just 14 years old, Tyson weighed 190lbs and had the body of a man. However, his mind was far from developed and Cus knew this would be the deciding factor if he was to become a champion.

To help, Cus began building Tyson's self-esteem. He would talk to him at night, after a hard day's training, feeding his mind with positive suggestions. Tyson recalls that,

> As time was going on, this guy would keep saying these great things about me. I didn't know if this guy was queer. He just kept saying great things about me. He would say, "You're a great fighter. You're the greatest. You're doing splendid, you look great." He just kept giving me compliments about everything I did.

> So, what's wrong with this guy? I never had the slightest idea he was building up my confidence. But, as time went on, I understood what he was doing. As I became an adult, I understood he was building up my confidence.

Can you see the formula at work? An *authority figure* (a trainer who has already produced champions), *repeatedly* (every night) tells his student about his potential. He communicates this message with *intensity* (because it's his genuine belief) and, as a result, the student starts to believe. The rest was history. Tyson cut a swathe through the heavyweight division, becoming the youngest ever champion (a record which still stands to this day) at the age of 20.

What can *you* expect when using the powerful triumvirate of authority, intensity and repetition to access the power of belief? Your life will change in incredible ways. To get an idea of the power you'll be tapping into, read the stories of these two different people who, off the back of a powerful childhood beliefs, rose to the heights of their respective professions.

Paul Mckenna is a renowned hypnotist, self-help author and speaker. He first made his mark on UK television and radio audiences in the early 1990s and, from there, went from strength to strength. Becoming an NLP master practitioner was a natural progression for this hypnotist and, when he combined forces with NLP's founder, Richard Bandler, a series of best-selling books and sell out seminars followed.

Some people might display a false modesty when discussing their success. Fortunately, Mckenna doesn't. He was quite frank in an interview with the Sunday Times Magazine in January 2017, when he told a reporter,

> I always just knew I was going to be famous, so I started practising my autograph when I was seven. I thought I was going to be James Bond or a drummer.

Beliefs become reality. With countless TV shows (in the 1990s), 17 published books and a net worth of £65 million, McKenna became his belief. Of course, he was neither James Bond nor a drummer, but the belief he would be famous led him to the avenue best suited to make this happen.

Napoleon Bonaparte shared a similar story. Despite humble beginnings, he nurtured an amazing sense of destiny about himself. The British publisher, Conrad Black, in his review of the book, *Bonaparte*, mentions,

> No matter how much anyone may have read on the subject, this book will provide some new insights into how Napoleon became convinced of, and clung to, his belief in his exalted and exceptional destiny through many years of obscurity and indifference or even mockery at the hands of his young French peers.[19]

Part of this belief, according to legend and documented in Claude Bristol's book, *The Magic of Believing*, was created when he was given a sapphire by a gypsy, as a small boy, and told he would one day be Emperor of France.

At the time, this was an unlikely prophecy. Napoleon was born in Corsica and was not of noble birth. However, he held onto this belief and, what would have appeared impossible to everyone else, became his reality.

What will you use the power of belief to achieve? There are no limits to what you can accomplish so choose something you are both passionate about and that brings meaning to your life.

When making this choice, remember one last rule. It would be a mistake to ask, "when is this going to happen?" or wonder why it's taking so long. This displays *a lack of belief* in the process. Instead, you must adopt the outlook that it happens *now*.

There is no space or time when impressing a belief on your subconscious. It's not like the physical realm, where growth occurs over a period of months or years. Instead, everything that has ever happened, and is going to happen, is happening now. Therefore, assume you *already are* whatever it is you want to be. Don't make the mistake of viewing your success as far off in the future, for it will always remain so. However, if you say, "*I am* the owner of a company with a million dollar a year turnover," or, "I have enough coaching clients to make $10,000 a month," then you allow the power of belief to work.

Say this even if your company hasn't launched yet and you haven't even secured your first client. Say it and think it, and it will become so.

Why you must avoid the over thinking trap

Whilst it's important you monitor and regulate your thoughts; it would be a mistake to remain entirely in your head. There are times when you must feel rather than think. Furthermore, there are some mental habits you must avoid.

Those of an analytical disposition are prone to overthinking. When faced with a problem, they will endlessly ruminate on the cause of their situation. Like trying to find the perfect outfit for a night out, they'll "try on" different explanations or theories.

Perhaps it was something in their past and if they can just understand the root cause then they can be free. Or, perhaps they should try a new approach or tactic. There must be a secret to success, that one piece of information they're missing, that will bring them their desired outcome. So, they think about their problem from one angle, and then another, experimenting with different theories but, ultimately, remaining stuck.

If you recognise any of these symptoms then I want you to remember a quote from the creator of Gestalt Therapy, Fritz Pearls. Back in 1951, he was advising clients to, "Lose your mind and come to your senses" - an instruction that steers you away from endlessly searching for an answer in your head.

This is such effective advice because rumination only leads you deeper into the overthinking trap. Compare your mind to quick sand. When you become trapped by a particular problem or issue, it's very tempting to struggle. You think about it, over and over, believing that by dwelling on it, you might figure out what's going wrong and, thereby, find a solution. However, what you don't realise is that, by giving attention to your problem, you're dragging yourself deeper into the issue.

This is the quick sand of your mind and, to escape, you must stop thinking and start living. Go out into the world and let it awaken your senses. Live and experience. Take action. The subsequent perspective you gain will provide a solution enabling you to move on.

Thomas Edison explained this seemingly counter intuitive phenomena when he said, "Great ideas originate in the muscles." They don't come through hours spent thinking through different options in your mind. Instead, they arrive when you consciously let go and engage with the activities of the day. Then, while using your muscles (doing something) your subconscious will present you with a great idea.

This occurs because the act of engaging in an activity raises your energy. When you're feeling more upbeat, positive energy and ideas start to flow. This process will present you with a solution that will alleviate your suffering. However, you must give yourself the mental space needed for it to occur.

Ironically, doing nothing at all is often a far better strategy than dwelling on your problems. You might feel you're giving up, but you're actually demonstrating faith in your subconscious's ability to rectify your situation. As a result, in time, a solution will be presented.

Start to develop this kind of calm faith. Cease all worry and overthinking. Lose yourself in life and you'll find your way.

Why you shouldn't place limits on your thinking

Perhaps your dreams are on an epic scale. Like Elon Musk, you have visions so great you imagine you can create new worlds. Or, like Michael Jackson, you believe you can fly (He was once quoted saying, "We can fly, you know. We just don't know how to think the right thoughts and levitate ourselves off the ground.")

Crazy, right? These kinds of people are unhinged and don't live in "the real world." However, look at what they accomplish.

Elon Musk's SpaceX created the first privately developed rocket to carry a commercial satellite into orbit. Michael Jackson, despite being told by everyone around him that it was impossible, created the greatest selling album of all time. So, are they crazy for having outrageous dreams or is this kind of thinking a prerequisite for achieving goals that seem out of the ordinary?

We're always being told about our limits. According to society, so much is impossible. For example, for a long time, it was deemed physically impossible for a human to run a mile in under 4 minutes. However, since Roger Bannister broke that limit in 1955, over 500 people, in America alone, have matched this feat.

In Arnold's Schwarzenegger's autobiography, *Total Recall*, he mentions that

> In weight lifting, for many years there was a 500-pound barrier in the clean and jerk . . .But as soon as the great Russian weightlifter Vasily Alekseyev set a new world record of 501 in 1970, three other guys lifted more than 500 pounds within a year.[20]

Another limit gets broken. How much proof do people need before they'll open their minds to the idea there are no limits (or, that's it's not useful to think of them)?

Michael Jackson claimed humans have the capacity to fly through the power of thought. Is this crazy? Of course, to date, no one has been recorded achieving this feat. And, perhaps, no one ever will. However, cast your thoughts back to the mind-set of a human living 600 years ago, ponder the possibility of machine powered flight from this perspective, and you'll see that you're presented with a similar situation.

Back then, if someone had said that humanity will crisscross the skies in giant flying machines within 600 years, it would have been considered utterly impossible. However, fast forward to today, and this is our reality.

Do you get the point? For the so-called impossible to occur, it takes people with a mind-set like Michael Jackson and Elon

Musk. Such a person, living 600 years ago, would have been interested, rather than dismissive, about the possibility of machine powered flight. As a result of this curiosity, research would have been undertaken, prototypes built and, as the centuries passed, and other illuminated minds continued their work, actual flight would finally occur.

A similar situation might occur with thought-powered flight. Or, it might not. Whatever the case, it serves no purpose to dismiss ideas on the grounds that they challenge the paradigms of our day. For, as we have seen with the examples of Jackson and Musk, thinking outside society's limitations is beneficial for both the individual and for humanity.

To achieve *your* dream, you must let your imagination soar. Allow yourself to contemplate the so called impossible, go to possibilities in your mind that have never been conceived before and, by doing so, unlock your full potential.

Never say that something can't be done. What's the point? If it can't, then you're no worse off than before. If it can, you could be the one breaking new ground while everyone stares in amazement.

CHAPTER 6: VITAL SKILLS TO BECOME OUTSTANDING

What skills will you need as you continue your journey to creating the life you want?

Undoubtedly, creativity will be one. Typically, we tend to think of this quality only being used by artists, designers and story tellers. However, did you ever consider that creativity might be the ability to solve problems or find unique ways to teach or communicate a message?

Routines and habits, although not as glamorous as creativity and genius, are the foundations upon which an outstanding life, and person, are built. Therefore, you must learn how to establish effective ones and break those that are either destructive or not working.

Finally, perhaps the greatest indicator of someone who has discovered their greatness is an ability to perform under pressure. This skill reveals a person.

Do they truly believe in themselves, and their destiny, or are they playing at becoming great? Those that are genuine, will rise to the occasion, sometimes delivering a superior performance because of the pressure they face. However, those that don't, can always improve and learn what is needed to reach these heights.

Finally, you'll want to learn these news skills quickly. Learning "how to learn" can be just as important as the skill you acquire. This, you will be taught, as you equip yourself with everything you need to become outstanding.

How to Reconnect with your Genius

Research indicates that, as we get older, we lose touch with our genius. Worryingly, it appears to be conditioned out of us.

Bryan Mattimore talks about this in his book, *21 Days to a Big Idea*. He references a famous 10-year study into creativity conducted by futurist and author, George Land.

In this study, a group of five-year olds took the NASA creativity test and then, ten years later, were tested again. Mattimore describes the findings as both startling and depressing. When the children were five years old, 98% of them scored at the highest level for creativity. At age ten, the percentage of children in this category had dropped to 30%. At age 15, the figure was 12%.

What could account for such a precipitous drop in creativity? It was clear to the researches that school, and the emphasis on getting the single "right answer," was to blame. As educator Neil Postman said, "children enter schools as question marks, and leave as periods."[21]

These findings are fascinating. It's amazing to think that, at 5 years old, almost all children are creative geniuses. It's also clear what causes them to lose their powers. The school system teaches them to become rational, logical thinkers. Creativity is seen as something without purpose in the "real world." It's not going to pay the bills, so why bother wasting time developing it?

But what if you want to keep your genius level of creativity? Even if you're not a writer, painter or inventor, you'll still need good ideas for selling a product, persuading potential customers and improving productivity.

If you're looking to reconnect with your genius, the good news is that it can never be destroyed. No matter how much it's neglected, it's always there, waiting to be tapped. However, to do so, you must follow a couple of important steps.

First, *you must listen*. Your creativity will speak to you in flashes of inspiration. These are usually accompanied by feelings of excitement. You might be working away on a problem, consciously engaged in finding a solution, and then you take a break. As you do, engaging your mind in a different, more mundane, activity (like getting some water or washing your dishes), suddenly, a new idea hits you. Boom! You see a solution and the realisation makes you feel great.

This is your genius speaking. Your excitement lets you know the idea you've had, or understanding you've come to, is important. Therefore, don't let it be forgotten. Make sure you write it down or record it.

This is an important step. The ideas your genius presents you with are so specific to the moment you're intuiting them, that unless you record them, it can be difficult to get into the same state and remember exactly what they revealed.

In Richard Branson's book, *Business Stripped Bare*, he gives a behind the scenes look at, and history of, his entrepreneurial career. Insights are shared from all his different ventures, from Virgin Music, to Virgin Galactic but perhaps the biggest takeaway is the importance Branson places on note taking. Throughout the course of a day, or working week, he'll have many ideas for his different businesses and to ensure he captures them, a notebook is constantly by his side.

Your genius might speak to you with a title for a new book, blog post or video. It could be the solution to an equation you're working on. It could be how an intricate part of new invention is going to fall into place. Whatever it is, you don't want to miss it, so record it on your phone or write it down.

Once your genius has spoken, don't overanalyse the insight it reveals. Instead, give your creativity free reign and see where it leads. Carry out the prompt without doubt or criticism. Be like a child. Act spontaneously and with limited self-awareness.

This is how to reconnect with your genius. If 95% of five-year olds possess this quality then you must emulate their approach.

Don't be embarrassed by the prospect of doing this. Furthermore, realise that, sometimes, your genius will alert you to an idea that comes to nothing. On other occasions, it will present you with the winning answer. Whatever the case, keep connecting with it and acting on its promptings. Be brave enough to resist the critical part of your mind and you'll reconnect with a brilliance that could rapidly transform your life.

Why it's so difficult to break habits and how to approach change

Mark Twain once said, "To promise not to do a thing is the surest way in the world to make a body want to go and do that very thing."

Why is that? Why is it that when you tell yourself you won't smoke, or snack or overeat anymore, or that you won't fail at a certain activity, you just keep doing it?

If this is the case for you then you need to understand that your subconscious can't process a negative. By telling yourself you're not going to do something; *you're still thinking about it.* Therefore, even though your intentions are true, you're fanning the flames of desire.

The more you think about something, the more you want it. Because of this psychological rule, rather than thinking about what you want to avoid, think about what you want to become. For example, if you want to stop smoking, start thinking about how much healthier you'll be. Consider the wonder of your taste buds regaining their senses and you enjoying your food. Imagine your fitness improving and see yourself enjoying taking part in a sport.

Or, you might be motivated by something else. Perhaps a new identity appeals the most. You see yourself as strong and self-reliant and that's why being dependent on cigarettes no longer has a place in your life. Whatever the case, focus on the thing you want, not what you're seeking to move away from.

Programme your mind in this manner and it won't be long before you leave old habits behind. Don't fight them. Remember, they're kept alive by your attention. French psychologist Emile Coue once said, "When the imagination and willpower are in conflict, it is always the imagination that wins, without any exception." This is because when you focus on something (even telling yourself you won't do it), the subconscious assumes you want more. As a result, it generates the cravings that correspond to its instructions and you end up trapped in the willpower loop.

A more productive approach would be ceasing all thought related to the habit you want to change. This alone will drastically reduce the cravings. Then, soon after, focus on what you want to become. These two approaches combined will eliminate the unwanted behaviour.

Sometimes this change happens immediately and, sometimes, it's a lengthier process. The problem is that *thinking about what you don't want* is instinctive. We're programmed to *fight* threats, as seen with our fight or flight reflex.

Societies conditioning doesn't help either. It teaches us to force things through and use willpower. The alternative, letting go and focusing on what you want, is counter intuitive. Therefore, this skill might need to be learned.

Give yourself time during this process. Be understanding if you slip back into old ways. Eventually, your subconscious will heed the message and the change will occur.

How to learn new skills quickly

Can you remember getting a new computer game as a child? Did you take the cartridge out, set it aside, and study the instruction manual for 30 minutes? Or, did you rip the game out of its packaging, hurriedly insert it in the console, and start playing?

Stupid question, right? Nothing was going to stop you getting straight to the action. In the process, you tested the buttons, made different movements with the directional control and soon discovered how to navigate your way through the game. The manual was there if you needed it but, mainly, you were learning through experience.

Now, imagine you explored the manual *before* you played the game. This would have been a completely different approach to learning. Invariably, with no reference point, the instructions were difficult to understand. Plus, there were too many of them. This led to confusion. You'd start up the game, after 30 minutes of study, and robotically try to make your way through the levels. However, your ass was getting kicked because you couldn't remember the right buttons to press and were spending too much time thinking instead of reacting.

How does this computer game analogy relate to the way you learn skills in the wider context of your life? While it's likely you learned to play computer games instinctively, it's unlikely you follow this approach with other areas. You don't jump straight in and "learn on the move." Instead, you'll spend a long-time seeking information. You'll take courses, read books and, perhaps, hire a coach.

While there's nothing wrong with doing so, and all can be valuable sources of information, 'seeking information' *before* taking action might mean you struggle when putting your knowledge to use. The reason for this is interesting. *To perform to the best of your ability, you must be present. You must deal with what's in front of you rather than following a predefined approach.*

This is why "learning on the move" can be so effective. It's explorative and fun. You're feeling, not thinking. As a result, you're seeing opportunities and answers, as if by magic, come to you.

While following the "seeking information" approach, this won't occur. Here, you might freeze up when faced with a practical situation because your mind is overloaded. This is because you can only consciously process approximately 7 (plus or minus 2) bits of information at any one time.[22] Therefore, bombarding your mind with a load of theory, facts and figures, and then trying to recall all of that when needing to perform, is a recipe for disaster.

Ultimately, there is no way to avoid failure while you learn. You'll experience this outcome regardless of the approach you take. However, at least when "learning on the move," you fail fast and recover from your mistakes quickly.

By contrast, failure while following the "seeking information" approach is frustrating. You know how things should work but, for some reason, they don't happen in the way the textbook or course explains.

This sometimes leads to an even greater quest for information. As a result of your frustration, you're convinced there must be some extra piece of knowledge to acquire and spend further hours attending more courses or reading books. However, all along, you fail to realise that if you just engaged with the activity you're learning, without any preconceived notions of how it should work, you'll naturally start to discover answers.

Remember, the manual, course, book or coach will always be there when you need to consult them. In fact, sometimes they're very useful. You can supercharge your learning with focused consultation sessions. However, these are most effective *after* some practical experience as it brings a deeper insight into the diagrams, theories and methodology.

Finally, you must be careful not to go too far in the other direction and completely ignore all instructions, courses and coaching. This is a mistake. Remember, it's not that acquiring information from third party sources is wrong. Far from it. It's just that the order in which you're trying to learn needs to be reversed. Go back to your computer playing days. Play. Consult. Improve. Keep repeating that cycle and you can master anything.

How to perform under pressure

Whether it's a product you're selling, a match you're attempting to win, an important speech you have to deliver or an interview for a new job, pressure situations are unavoidable. Ironically, in practice or rehearsal, when the pressure is off, you might deliver a perfect performance. However, when you believe it matters, your nerves attack and prevent you from relaxing and letting everything flow.

If you've ever had this experience, then there are three things you need to learn.

The first concerns your preparation. Studies indicate that we only have conscious control over 2% - 4% of our actions, decisions and behaviour. The other 96% - 98% is subconscious.[23] This means that, when faced with a pressure situation, we have very little ability to *directly* influence the outcome.

On the surface, this may seem a reason to be even more nervous. However, with deeper analysis, this statistic is liberating.

If you did have 100% conscious control over your actions, decisions and behaviour then you would perform exactly as you pleased. There would be no forgetting lines, singing out of tune or slicing the shot. Unfortunately, your mind doesn't work this way. Instead, the route to control is through the subconscious. It's not a case of *willing* yourself to perform, it's about *programming* yourself to do so.

What does this mean? You should focus on where you *can* make an impact. Muhammad Ali once said, "The fight is won or lost far away from witnesses - behind the lines, in the gym, and out there on the road, long before I dance under those lights."

Ali is letting you know that what you *bring* into a pressure situation is more important (96% to 98%) than what you *do* in a pressure situation. Therefore, all your attention should go into making sure your preparation is as comprehensive as possible.

At the start of my speaking career, I spoke in front of an audience of 40 people. In retrospect, this was a small crowd but, up until that point, I'd never spoken to an audience larger than 10. As a result, I felt under pressure. I'd built up the occasion in my mind and told myself that I had to deliver.

Going in, I didn't have much experience to rely on. Therefore, to ensure I maximized the 96% impact my subconscious was going to have, I knew I needed to go overboard with my preparation.

I was allocated a 10-minute slot, although without recourse to slides or notes. In preparation, I spent 10 hours conceptualising, writing and then rehearsing my talk.

It paid off. Barring one moment where I very briefly forgot what to say, the talk flowed and was met with overwhelmingly positive feedback.

I include this example to give you some idea of the length of time needed to perform successfully when faced with a pressure situation. Ten hours for ten minutes was the ratio I used. Of course, if you've got experience then you can often cut down on your preparation time by more than half. This is because experience *is* preparation, quite possibly the best kind. However, if you don't, then be prepared to put in the hours.

If you do, you'll find that, even though you might be feeling one or two nerves, your preparation will carry you through the performance to a successful conclusion. This is why having very little conscious control over the performance is, in some way, liberating. There's not much you can change (2% to 4%) once you're up there on the stage, sitting in front of your potential future boss or standing on the court. So, why worry? If you've done your preparation then just let the rest flow.

The second key to performing under pressure is letting go. Even the most meticulous preparation has the potential to be sabotaged by anxiety in the days and hours leading up to the event. Thoughts about the consequences of failure will alter your voice and body language, make you forget what you planned to say and impair your judgment.

To perform successfully, you need to be calm and relaxed enough for everything to flow. In order for this to happen, you must learn to *live in the now*.

Rarely are your fears rooted in reality. Instead, they're based on something that happened in the past or a potential event you fear in the future. Therefore, they are not real and, if you're always present, you can't be affected.

Of course, living in the now is easier said than done. Doing so requires a tremendous amount of vigilance and patience. You have to monitor your thoughts and be aware of the moments when your mind dwells on the fear of the future or regrets from the past.

Typically, this might occur during your preparation time. It's an obvious trigger point so be hyper vigilant in these moments. Then, when you're engaged with other activities (cooking, cleaning, travelling etc), *completely switch off*. Forget about the upcoming event.

Living in the now takes time to master but, keep practicing, and the fear will eventually clear. It has to. Your thoughts are the only thing keeping it alive!

The final key to performing under pressure is changing your mindset. Even if you're a beginner, you must adopt the mindset of a master. Ask yourself the following questions;

- How would a master *feel* in the moments leading up to the talk, match or pitch?
- How would they carry themselves or use their voice when speaking?
- How would they feel the night before the important event?
- What kind of energy do they bring to what they're doing?

For example, does a master tremble with nerves the night before an important event and find it impossible to sleep? No, they've done it a thousand times before and believe in themselves to such a degree they feel calm. Does a master mumble and look at their feet when required to deliver an important message? No, they feel comfortable, stand tall and project their voice throughout the room.

By putting yourself in the mind of a master you now have a direction to follow and a standard by which you can measure yourself. It doesn't matter if you're a complete beginner and, initially, struggle to meet this standard. It's always there for you to aim towards and prevent you from drifting into negative thinking.

When using this technique, don't tell yourself that you're "faking it" or that it isn't "true." Few people are naturals, performing without any nerves and little preparation. We must all go through a process. Part of it is putting yourself in the mindset of the performer you want to become and imagining that you have their confidence until you do.

With these three techniques – preparation, living in the now and altering your mindset – you are now ready to perform to the best of your ability. Embrace the stage (or whatever arena you perform in). It's your opportunity to share your truth, message or gift with the world, so make the most of it.

CHAPTER 7: DAILY PRACTISES FOR PEAK PERFORMANCE

To achieve high levels of performance, day in, day out, you need to regulate your thoughts and mood. This can be hard to achieve while rushing from your home, to your place of work, and bouncing from one task to another. That's why you must take time away from your hectic schedule to refresh and focus your mind. Solitude and space are required. The ability to trigger positive feelings of inspiration, happiness and certainty must be developed.

All of this takes practise. It won't always come easily. This is why you need a routine to support you.

In this chapter, I'll be discussing some of the most effective ones I've created for both myself and my clients. All of them involve tapping into the power of your subconscious mind. There, deep in the recesses of your connection with the universal intelligence, answers will be revealed, issues will be resolved and anxieties will be released.

How to use meditation and self-hypnosis to rid yourself of anxiety and program your mind for success

Two incredibly useful practices to build into your daily routine are meditation and self-hypnosis. I recommend you spend 5 minutes a day on both.

The following is my definition of how to perform each practice. You may perform them differently and that's fine. The important thing is the consistency with which you practise and that your approach brings the desired results.

If it's not, then study the following instructions and put them to use. Both disciplines, once applied consistently, have the power to change your life in dramatic and positive ways.

MEDITATION

PURPOSE: To clear your mind of anxious, stressful, unnecessary, distracting thoughts.

BENEFIT: Enables you to be present, whether working on something important, competing or spending times with loved ones. Therefore, improves performance and increases enjoyment.

HOW TO: Set aside 5 minutes each day (although don't clock watch) where you won't be disturbed. Sit down. (This is preferable to lying down as you might fall asleep). Make sure you're comfortable and then close your eyes.

Focus on your breathing. Don't try to DO anything with your thoughts or think about anything in particular (the object is to empty your mind). Just keep focusing on your breathing.

At some point, a thought will pop into your head. If it does, just release it and bring your attention back to your breathing.

This may happen a lot at the start. That's fine. Just keep bringing your attention back to your breathing. After the 5 minutes is over, get up and continue your day.

As you continue with your practice, you'll develop the ability to free your mind of unwanted or distracting thoughts. It might be frustrating at first and far from relaxing. Your mind might race with hundreds of different thoughts. That's ok. You're learning. The most important thing is that you stick with it.

Eventually, you'll reach a point where these thoughts become less frequent and then a wonderful sense of peace will come over you. Not only that, you'll be able to take this calm into your daily life and apply it to different situations. Fear or distraction may arise but, with wonderful precision, you'll be able to bring yourself back to the present and the unwanted thought or feeling will disappear.

SELF-HYPNOSIS

PURPOSE: To provide you with useful insights and access to empowering emotional states (e.g., confidence).

BENEFIT: During your day-to-day life, answers, in the form of hunches or intuitions will be revealed which, if followed, will guide you on your journey to success. Allows you to feel positive, or uplifted (or any state you choose), on command (this takes a lot of practise).

HOW TO: As with meditation, set aside 5 minutes in a comfortable, quiet place. Light a candle and stare at the flame. Alternatively, find a fixed and small object you can stare at (a hook on the wall works well or anything no larger than a few inches). Try to have the object or candle above your line of sight so that you're staring upwards.

Before you start, set an objective for your session. What are you working towards at the moment? Is it selling a certain number of units? Is it gaining 3 extra clients a week? Or, perhaps it's losing a certain amount of weight. Whatever it might be, make sure you are certain of the end goal. Alternatively, if your objective is to develop a particular emotional state (for example, joy) then be clear on this before you start.

Then, once your objective is set, just fix your gaze on the candle or the object you've selected. It may take two minutes, or a few more but, at some point, you'll find yourself slowing down and your eyes will get heavy. At this point, let them shut.

With your eyes closed, fix your thoughts on your end goal (e.g., 3 extra clients a week or feeling confident). Then, visualise different scenarios in your mind where this goal is realised. For example, imagine the clients in your office and see the extra money in your account. Also, see the sessions going well. Imagine your client's issues being resolved and them recommending you to friends. Notice how amazing this feels.

If it's confidence you seek, imagine yourself acting with this feeling in a relevant situation. Then, notice where you feel it in your body. From this epicentre, imagine it pulsating through the rest of your body so the confidence radiates from you. If other thoughts flash through your mind (and they will, especially during the early stages), keep bringing your attention back to your objective.

The most important part of self-hypnosis is building an emotional connection with what you're imagining. Triggering this response lets you know your subconscious is accepting the images you're supplying. Therefore, make everything feel as real as possible.

Remember feeling absorbed by a dream you had at night or watching a movie. Neither of these experiences could, technically, be described as "real" yet both trigger deep emotions. Successful self-hypnosis is the same.

Once you've completed 5 minutes, open your eyes and continue with your day. Then, expect answers. At some point, when your mind isn't actively engaged, a hunch may pop into your head, revealing an idea or answer that, if pursued, will advance your life. This is your subconscious responding to the successful programming of your self-hypnosis. It will do the same with your desired emotional states, triggering the required feeling at the appropriate time.

Why 5 minutes? Of course, you can choose to do more if you prefer and an effective 20-minute meditation or self-hypnosis session is more impactful than a 5 minute one. However, I suggest 5 minutes because it can become a part of your daily routine.

Everyone can commit 5 minutes a day to something important. When you're busy, 20 minutes is harder to find. There's more chance you'll skip your meditation, or self-hypnosis, and tell yourself you'll catch up tomorrow. However, if you get in the habit of taking a day off, it then becomes easier to justify missing another day (and then another). Then, before you know it, you're not meditating or practising self-hypnosis at all.

It's for this reason that 5 minutes a day is recommended. You can do it every day and the momentum this builds will change your life.

What I learned from practising self-hypnosis every day, for a year

In 2016, I undertook a challenge. I decided to practise self-hypnosis *every single day* of the year. I'd set myself this goal the previous two years running. However, on both occasions, I failed to manage the events in my life and couldn't complete the challenge.

This time, though, I knew exactly what I was facing. I knew how to avoid repeating previous mistakes and make sure I was successful. 365 days later, I was.

There were close calls (pulling my car over to the side of the road to get a session in at 11.50pm, and having to break off phone conversations with my girlfriend to ensure I didn't miss the midnight deadline) but there wasn't a day that went by without me sticking to this practise. Mentally and spiritually stronger, I now share my experiences with you.

My aim in doing so is that you might take up a similar challenge. You may already practise meditation or self-hypnosis but how consistent are you? Do you have a routine or is it sporadic?

The great thing about undertaking a challenge is the increased motivation it brings. Ordinarily, there may be days when you don't feel like meditating or practising self-hypnosis. When there are no consequences for skipping, it can be all too easy to let these slide. However, if the consequences are failing your challenge, it's more likely you'll push through and stick to the practice.

This is why I'm encouraging you to set your own challenge. Learn from my example and create something suited to your needs. A year later, you'll feel stronger and proud of yourself for having followed through.

There were 12 lessons I learned from completing my challenge. Before I reveal them, it's important to clarify the focus of my self-hypnosis sessions. The practice itself was exactly the same as described in the previous section. During the sessions, I would focus my mind on selling one million copies of my books. I would visualise the number 1,000,000 in my mind or rehearse a scene whereby, after having sold the requisite amount, I revisited my old University (the site of my greatest unhappiness) and celebrated by returning to the significant places of my time there (to me, this represented a moment of triumph over adversity). Another significant visual was imagining myself having sold a million copies and celebrating under a waterfall, with my arms raised above my head, reaching out to the sky.

These were the three main visualisations I used. Alongside them, there were a few secondary ones. No matter how low my sales were, I always had a short to medium term target in mind. For example, when I first published my book, it was getting just 1 sale. After that, it was 100. When that was accomplished, it was 1000.

At the time of undertaking the challenge, I had sold approximately 400. Therefore, my focus was on 1000 book sales. However, I would also glance beyond that and imagine reaching 10,000.

Connecting with my readers was also important. I would imagine people from different parts of the world reading my first book *Escape The System* and having some kind of revelation doing so. Using the feeling I've had when reading a book that was important to me, I would imagine my readers being touched in a similar way.

The purpose of these self-hypnosis sessions was to programme my mind with the idea that I was a best-selling author. I knew that if I could do this, then my subconscious would bring about this reality.

When it came to the rules of the challenge, I had to perform one self-hypnosis session every day, for approximately 10 minutes. Furthermore, this had to be completed before midnight. If I went one minute over, it was a fail.

As a result of completing the challenge, I learned the following lessons. They apply whether you choose to do self-hypnosis, meditation or a mixture of the two.

1. There is no perfect time to practise.
Sometimes I did it first thing in the morning, sometimes it was last thing at night. Occasionally, I even did it during the day. It made no difference to the effectiveness of the self-hypnosis. Practise is what gets you good at focusing your mind, not doing it at a particular time.

2. Practising every day requires a surprising amount of planning.
If you're out early in the morning, you may not have time to complete your session before work. A busy job may prevent you from doing it during the day. Being tired at night, or going out with friends, may stop you from getting it done before you go to bed.

To prevent this from happening you must plan, either the day before or when you wake up in the morning, when you'll do your 10 minutes. You can set a timer on your phone, record it in a diary or, if your memory is good and you're accustomed to practising daily, then make a mental note.

3. There will be times when you don't feel like doing it.

Throughout the course of a 365-day year, there are going to be moments (perhaps many) when you feel tired. There are going to be occasions when you feel demotivated or receive bad news. In these moments, the thought of completing your meditation or self-hypnosis will be unappealing. However, this is when the practise shows its true value.

You may have thought this challenge is about calming, or focusing, your mind. While this occurs, it's not the main benefit of completing the challenge. Where you're really growing is in willpower and self-discipline. By practising when you don't want to, you gain mastery over the weaker elements of your mind. Expect to see knock on effects in areas like controlling your eating, going to the gym and working on your project or business.

4. Practising a little bit each day is more powerful than infrequent marathon sessions.

This also applies to exercise, diet or any habit change you want to create. Success is largely about momentum. The most effective way to create this is to do something regularly.

5. These 10 minutes are the most important of your day.

We're conditioned into thinking the job interview, or the exam, or the first date are the most important moments in our lives. However, the way these events play out is largely a reaction to our subconscious programming. That's why these 10 minutes a day should be considered sacred and *given precedence over everything else.*

6. Make a note of each day you complete

This is a great way to stay motivated. Celebrate each successful day by noting it down. Tick off in a diary or use an app to keep track of your progress. You'll notice that you look forward to marking it down and, by doing so, you're motivated to continue the challenge.

7. Sometimes it will feel like hard work.

Meditation and self-hypnosis aren't always fun. Stopping your thoughts from wandering can feel like hard work. This is because the lazy part of your mind is fighting with your higher self. Don't let it win by permitting your mind to wander. Keep returning your thoughts to the focus of your session. Eventually, your mind will obey.

8. The more you do it, the easier it gets.

The good news is, it gets easier. After three months, doing 10 minutes of self-hypnosis a day was no longer a hassle. By six months, I was looking forward to my daily sessions. Expect to experience a similar change.

9. You will become mentally and spiritually stronger.

As a result of meditating daily, you will be more relaxed and your mood will naturally raise. Self-hypnosis will harness the power of focus to help you achieve your goals. Irrespective of which one you're practising; your discipline and willpower will improve. Furthermore, when times get tough, and you're faced with some kind of adversity, the daily practice will shield you from panic and ensure you maintain your equilibrium.

10. Every session doesn't have to be successful.

For me, a successful session was as follows. I silence my wandering mind. Then, I gained an emotional connection with the object of my focus (feeling ecstatic about selling 1 million copies of my books). Once complete, I walked away feeling refreshed and positive.

It's important for you to know, especially if you're a beginner, that this won't always happen. Sometimes you'll sit down, close your eyes and, for most of the 10 minutes, your mind will wander. Then, when you open your eyes, you'll feel like you haven't accomplished anything.

Don't make the mistake of thinking this has been a wasted session. Even when you haven't built the desired emotional connection, you've still done something incredibly important.

You turned up! You displayed your commitment to grow and gave yourself the opportunity to be great. Don't underestimate how significant this is.

11. To complete the yearlong challenge, your 10-minute session must become one of your top priorities

Through my work as a hypnotherapist, I've witnessed many people being successful, and failing, at achieving their goals. The side of the divide *you* fall on, will have a lot to do with your priorities.

At the start of this section, I mentioned pulling my car over on a journey home at 11.50pm, and breaking off conversations with my girlfriend, to ensure I completed my daily self-hypnosis. Some people might consider these bizarre or selfish actions. However, if you're one of them, it's unlikely you'll be successful at completing your challenge.

What are your main priorities at the moment? Whether you enjoy it or not, one of them is probably your job. Another will be your husband/wife, boyfriend/girlfriend or children if you have them. Are you prepared to put this challenge alongside them in degrees of importance?

Sounds crazy, right? However, unless you do, it's almost certain you'll fail.

Inevitably, one of any number of scenarios will occur. Either, your mind might be so occupied with work commitments you'll forget to do your session. Or, your children staying up late, and being unable to sleep, will make you miss the midnight deadline. There are so many potential events and circumstances that could derail you. However, if they do, you have nothing, or no one, to blame.

You can always leave work 10 minutes early or, during your day, go and take a 10-minute break. Furthermore, you can leave your child alone for 10 minutes, irrespective of their protestations. Sure, there might be consequences to these actions but they won't be irreparable.

Whatever external circumstances you face, adopt the attitude that your 10 minutes *has* to be done. Everything else falls in around it. Perhaps an emergency, night-time visit to the hospital for a loved one trumps your challenge. However, then the question is, why didn't you complete your 10 minutes first thing in the morning?

Ultimately, there are no excuses or justifiable reasons why you can complete your daily self-hypnosis or meditation. You must *make* the time. In doing so, other areas of your life will have to be, at least temporarily, sacrificed. Understand and accept this situation.

12. You must have a strong "why" to complete the challenge.

It's very easy to get lax and skip a day when doing this challenge. To prevent this from happening, attach a powerful meaning to its success.

For me, it was about defining who I was as a person. Could I be the kind of person that excelled?

I'd always done well in school, at work and with sports, but never reached the highest levels. I gave 80% to 90% effort but never got to 100%.

That had to change. Instead of accepting my "80% is good enough" identity, I wanted to become a super achiever. The completion of the yearlong challenge was a big part of making this happen.

This reason undoubtedly helped me on the occasions I considered skipping a day. It fired me up because I was so determined to live up to my new identity. Find a similarly powerful reason and you *will* succeed.

How to set up a quick, daily motivational routine

You don't need to wake up at 5am, sacrifice sleep or spend an hour journaling, meditating and goal setting, to have an effective daily motivational routine. Instead, you can experience all the benefits in less than 10 minutes and at *any* time of day. Here's what to do.

1. Self-Hypnosis/Meditation

See above two sections for explanation.

Time taken to complete: 5 - 7 minutes

2. Reading personal statement or Definite Chief Aim

A personal statement is a short paragraph about what you want to achieve, written as if you've already achieved it. The subject matter could be anything. You might desire perfect health. If this is the case, you write about all your cells functioning perfectly and your body feeling full of energy. Or, perhaps you want your business to grow exponentially. If this is the case, you write about the number of new customers or clients you desire.

Repeat your statement three times over with as much passion and conviction as you can muster. Turn it into a performance, complete with dramatic gestures.

A Definite Chief Aim (DCA) is similar to a written statement. Created by Napoleon Hill and featured in *Think and Grow Rich*, it has four key components.

First, you must decide upon an amount of money you want to possess. Second, the date by which you are going to possess it. Third, what you are going to do in return for the money. Finally, once your DCA is written, repeat it out loud in the morning (upon waking) and again at night (before going to bed).

By way of example, here's Bruce Lee's DCA, written in 1969, *before* he became a worldwide star,

> I, Bruce Lee, will be the first highest paid Oriental superstar in the United States. In return I will give the most exciting performances and render the best quality in the capacity of an actor. Starting 1970, I will achieve world fame and from then onwards till the end of 1980 I will have in my possession $10,000,000. I will live the way I please and achieve inner harmony and happiness.[24]

Time taken to complete: 1 minute

3. Anchoring

This NLP technique enables you to form a connection between a physical movement and a powerful emotional feeling. For example, you might hold your arms aloft in the pose of a sports champion and connect this with a feeling of achievement. Or, you might simply press down with your right index finger on one of your left knuckles. While doing his, imagine yourself feeling completely relaxed and calm. This would be something very useful, and discreet, to use while giving a presentation.

When using this technique, the most important part is building the emotional connection. You need to *feel* something when you perform the movement. This may take time. However, once you've built the connection, anchoring only requires seconds of your day.

There are a variety of movements you can perform, depending on your situation and what works for you. On the tennis court, I like fist pumps. Before going to bed, I raise my hands above my head and imagine achieving all my goals. If no one is watching, I close both my eyes, clench my fists and imagine sending a burst of energy through my whole body.

Create your own movements based on the state you want to capture. A hand over your chest might soothe and calm you. Placing a finger to your temple might enhance focus. The more you repeat it, the stronger the connection becomes and the more accessible the state you desire. Eventually, you'll be able to anchor yourself for confidence, relaxation or energy, at will.

Time Taken to Complete: 30 secs

4. Create a motivational playlist

If you're pressed for time then why not use one of the most powerful emotional resources known to man - music! Our favourite songs aren't just entertainment. They carry deep meanings and trigger strong emotions in our limbic system.

So, get your phone or device and create a playlist of 10 or 20 of your most motivating songs. Then, play them at various times throughout the day.

The beauty of this technique is it can be completed while getting ready, tidying your house, travelling to work and training at the gym. Here are some of mine.

- Broken Wings - Mr. Mister
- A Change is Gonna Come - Sam Cooke
- Gonna Fly Now - Rocky theme song
- I Believe I can fly - R. Kelly
- Juicy - The Notorious B.I.G
- Keep the Faith - Michael Jackson
- Keep ya Head Up - 2Pac
- Slippin' - DMX
- Star Wars theme song

Time taken to complete: 0 – can be completed while engaged with other tasks.

5. The Victory Shout

You've probably noticed a reoccurring theme throughout this list - EMOTION. A good motivational routine should leave you feeling pumped and upbeat. There are few better ways of doing this than performing The Victory Shout.

The Victory Shout is a close cousin to the primal scream. Both involve the participant making a loud shout, released from the depths of their soul. (Think William Wallace in *Braveheart* after winning a battle or Novak Djokovic after winning a Grand Slam). When shouting, inject some passion into your voice and hold it for a few seconds.

Despite their similarities, The Victory Shout and the primal scream differ on one key component. The primal scream is used as a release from anger, frustration and pain. It has its roots in primal therapy, created by Arthur Janov, and is used as a means to overcoming repressed childhood trauma.

By contrast, The Victory Shout requires you to focus on the big goals you wish to achieve and the moment you realise them (selling 1 million copies of your books, paying off the mortgage on your dream home, finding and getting married to the love of your life). An intense connection will be made between yourself and the realisation of your desire when you perform the shout. To enhance the experience, close your eyes.

The Victory Shout represents the culmination of a lifetimes work and the incredible release of emotions that will occur once achieved. This intensity must be captured when you perform your shout (even though, technically, it hasn't happened and you're still working towards it). Being able to use your imagination in this way will give you a tremendous rush of energy and build a connection with your goal. Once performed, you'll feel certain of your chances for success.

Due to the nature of The Victory Shout, you may prefer to perform it when nobody else is around. I find that a dramatic, or scenic, location works best. The top of a hill, by the sea, in the woods, or even at significant monument, are all ideal. Of course, finding such a place is not always easy and, if you wish to perform this on a near daily basis, use the confines of your car.

Time Taken to Complete: 3-5 seconds.

So, there you have it. A motivational routine that will take you no longer than 10 or 12 minutes to complete and can be performed at any time of day. If you do it regularly, expect to experience increased energy, motivation and focus. You'll also be priming your subconscious to provide you with solutions to assist you on your journey.

As beneficial as this is, though, no routine can ever be entirely sacrifice free. Even 10 or 12 minutes out of your day can sometimes seem like a hardship when you've been busy and want to relax.

Push through these moments. Make yourself complete the routine. If you do, you'll discover a hidden benefit to completing these motivational techniques. Doing it daily forces you to turn up.

Woody Allen famously said, "80% of success is showing up." Keep reaffirming your commitment to living a greater life (by completing the routine) and you'll put yourself ahead of 95% of people who wish their lives got better but don't give any mental attention to this desire.

CHAPTER 8: STRENGTHEN YOUR SPIRIT TO OVERCOME ANY CHALLENGE

Throughout your journey to creating the life you want, there'll be decisive moments when the success of your endeavour seems to hang in the balance. Furthermore, there'll be times when you feel like you're pushing against a brick wall and need to breakthrough both the internal and external barriers standing in your way. On both occasions, you'll need to call on a power deep within you to reach the next level.

This power is intangible. You could call it your spirit or, if you're religious, you might call it God. It's both a source of wisdom and love and, to access it, you must know your "why."

You can also develop it by building a positive self-image. Noticing the progress you're making, rather than dwelling on the things that have gone wrong, is also essential as possessing this ability will help you face setbacks without losing sight of the bigger picture.

Courage is also essential. At many times throughout your journey, you're going to have to face your fears. Will you have the strength to do this? Day after day, will you be able to put yourself in situations that make you uncomfortable and expose your weaknesses?

If you build the strength necessary to do this, there's little that can stand in your way. *You* are the determining factor when it comes to your success. There's no power, outside of yourself, that can stop you. Read on to discover how to strengthen your spirit and soul.

Why having a positive self-image is so important

A few years ago, I went to a Muhammad Ali exhibition at the O2 arena in London. As I walked around, I was inspired. Not only was I dazzled by Ali's boxing prowess and career, I was awed by the strength he showed in standing up for what he believed in.

I left the venue in a state of deep thought. Many of Ali's quotes were plastered around the walls and most of them referenced his incredible self-belief. The one below was particularly thought provoking,

> Every man wants to believe in himself, and every man wants to be fearless. We become heroes when we stand up for what we believe in. Before I won the gold medal at the Olympics, before I became the heavyweight champion of the world, before I stood up to the United States government for my religious beliefs, before I was named a United Nations Ambassador of peace, and before I became the most recognised person in the world, I was just a kid from Kentucky who had the faith to believe in himself and the courage to follow his heart.

It's incredible to hear Ali talk about himself in this way. He was a kid from Kentucky who went on to conquer the world. How was he able to do this?

Of course, physical attributes and hard work played a massive role but there are plenty of other athletes who share these qualities. So, what was unique about Ali?

As seen below, Ali was the undisputed champion of positive self-image and talk.

"I'm the greatest of all-times."
"I'm so fast that last night I turned off the light switch in my hotel room and was in bed before the room was dark."
"I'm gonna show you how great I am."
"I'm the king of the world."

These were just some of the affirmations he would tell himself, his opponents and the media. Some were funny. Some seemed arrogant. All were fuelled by a certainty in himself and his abilities.

Compare them with the affirmations most people say and you'll notice a big difference.

"I'm rubbish at that."
"I'm not good enough."
"I couldn't do that."

In my country (I live in England), it's considered acceptable to talk about your weaknesses but a sign of thinking you're better than others if you vocalize a belief in yourself. How crazy is that? We encourage playing small in the misguided belief people will feel safe around us. Never do we think to express our greatness and, in doing so, give others permission to shine.

I doubt such an attitude is restricted to England. My country may be an extreme example, but how many cultures encourage positive self-talk?

Not many and this is the problem. You don't get to be great by telling yourself you're rubbish!

Two giants of the personal development world list identity, or self-image, as the main factor in determining an individual's level of success. Tony Robbins, with his best-selling books, seminars and celebrity roster of coaching clients, has this to say about identity, "Identity is the most important power that determines our actions. We will act according to our view of who we truly are - whether these views are accurate or not."[25]

Dr Maxwell Matlz, in his best-selling book, *Psycho-Cybernetics,* echoes these thoughts. He was originally introduced to the importance of self-image through his work as a plastic surgeon. After surgery, some of his clients were delighted with the results and adopted a more confident and outgoing persona. However, others experienced no change in their confidence levels despite their operation being a success.

This led him to the conclusion that *self-image was more important than actual image*. He could remove or correct what the patient viewed as an ugly disfigurement yet, if the patient still *saw* identified with being "ugly," then their self-esteem wouldn't change.

The relevance of these examples to Muhammad Ali is that we build our identity, or create a self-image, partly through self-talk. Tell yourself that you are "The Greatest" and you'll unleash your limitless potential. However, tell yourself that you're "not good enough" or "rubbish" or "ugly" and you'll unwittingly inflict a lifetime of self-sabotage on your efforts.

Of course, it might wear a little thin if you're constantly telling friends, colleagues and, anyone who'll listen, how amazing you are. Therefore, I suggest that you keep your positive self-talk to yourself. For example, anytime you're confronted with a work challenge, or are learning a new skill, you can gently remind yourself, "I can do this." When you're playing a match, or competing on any level, you can repeat the words, "I can win." Before you take to the stage to deliver a talk, or get up in front of your colleagues to give a presentation, you can tell yourself, "My words inspire."

There are hundreds of small phrases you can focus on to reinforce the message that you have the ability to achieve anything you desire. Of course, you have to *feel* them as well. Think back to how Ali used to talk about himself. He would shout and holler, "I'm the Greatest of all-times." In some interviews he looked manic, but it was this depth of feeling that turned mere words into a powerful identity. Evoke a similar level of intensity in your self-talk and you'll become what you say you are.

Why your perspective determines your success

Take a look at the picture below. Two characters are looking at planks of wood. One sees four, the other three. Who sees the situation correctly?

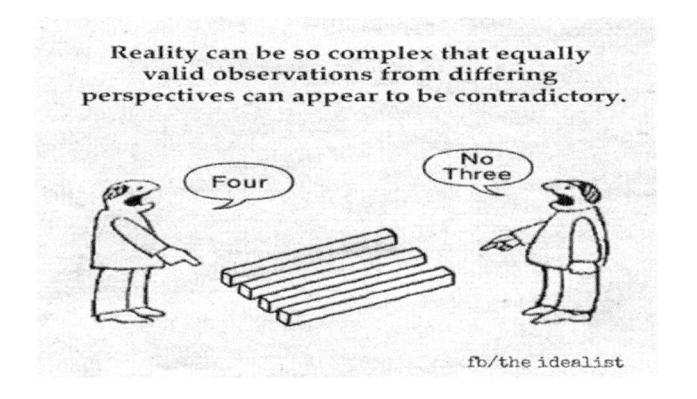

Reality can be so complex that equally valid observations from differing perspectives can appear to be contradictory.

fb/the idealist

Surprisingly, they both do because *the position you are in when looking at any object, or subject, will determine the view you take.*

You would agree with that statement, right? However, do you apply this logic to every area of your life? Do you have the ability to be that objective when measuring your own levels of success?

From over 10 years of working as a hypnotherapist, I would say that most of us don't. When it comes to evaluating ourselves, it's a case of absolutes.

- I can *never* overcome this problem
- I'm stuck
- I'm a failure

These are just some of the blanket statements I'll hear when meeting clients. While they could easily look at a dispute between other people and make an argument for why both parties had an equally compelling case, they can't look at their inner disputes and apply the same logic.

This is because, when it comes to themselves, they get emotional. The pain of past failure hits and blinds them from an alternative perspective. They forget all of the things they do well and mistake their negative perspective for the "truth."

As you can imagine, this has disastrous consequences for their quality of life. With this interpretation, they're battling something unalterable. There's no way around the fact they'll *forever* lack the confidence necessary to find a partner, the talent to excel at their work or the discipline to lose weight.

Does this ever happen to you? Do you find yourself unable to look at yourself, or your work, and find the positives? If so, there's something counter-intuitive you need to understand.

When it comes to *your* success, you're the one who determines the level.

To explain my point, I'm going to tell you a story about my book writing experience. I'm going to give you a very candid glimpse into my world and then I'm going to invite you to judge me. Am I a success or a delusional failure?

My dream is to sell a million copies of my books. I've had this dream for a long time and, at the time of writing, I've only sold 5500 copies.

So, what do you think? Clearly, I've failed, right? My goal is 1,000,000 and I'm at a measly 5500.

From one perspective, I can see how someone would think this way. The numbers are astronomically out and I've put in an inordinate amount of time (probably 10,000 hours including writing and promotional activities) for what would appear to be very little return. However, I can tell you now, hand on heart, that I feel anything but a failure.

Instead, I'm happy and I see myself, largely, as a success. This feeling is not just down to having sold twenty times more copies than the average self-published author (250, if you were wondering),[26] some fantastic reviews on Amazon and many people contacting me to share the positive impact my books have had on their lives. While these factors are incredibly rewarding, they could easily be washed away by the knowledge of what I *haven't* achieved.

I haven't been able to make a living from my writing and I'm so far away from my target it's laughable to suggest I might, one day, get there. Therefore, how can I justify seeing myself as a success?

The reason is the perspective I take. For over 17 years, I've trained myself to focus on the positives. Since July 2003, I've noted down, in a series of journals, every single significant positive result I've achieved. With time, I've built up a bank of evidence to support the idea that I'm successful.

Numerous tennis coaching and hypnotherapy clients have been acquired. I've helped people stop smoking, lose weight and free themselves from anxiety. Children I've coached have gone on to play tennis at national and regional level. Girlfriends have been gained when, once, all I experienced was rejection. Books have been sold. Positive feedback on my writing has been received. All of these results (and many more) have been documented and, although the failures outweigh the successes, not a single one of them features in my diaries.

As a result, I've conditioned my mind to latch onto the positives. Therefore, when I published my first book (back in 2012), and it took six weeks to sell its first copy to a non-family member, I didn't panic or fall apart. Instead, I waited to start achieving some results and then built on them.

While you might agree that my feelings of success are genuine, it would still be possible to argue that, ultimately, I'm deluding myself. I'm light years away from achieving my dream and if I persist, then what about the other areas of my life that are being neglected?

This is a legitimate concern. However, when questioned in this way, my response is always the same.

Focusing on the positives has turned my life around. Why would I stop now?

This discipline has seen me through the dark days and got me to the point where I know my books are marketable. Over the last year, I've more than doubled my sales and received a book deal for my second book, *Do The Work you Love*. None of this would have happened if I'd looked at my book sales and seen 994,500 failures instead of 5500 successes.

How many times have you looked at yourself negatively and, as a result, shut down the possibility of moving forwards? Furthermore, how much more will you achieve when you start to focus on the positives?

Realising you have this choice frees you from the grip of so called negative "truths." It puts you in the position to learn, improve and hang on long enough for an opportunity to come your way.

This is how winning is done. Failure is inevitable. That's why you don't focus on it. Learn from it. Never be ignorant and bury your head in the sand. However, never dwell on it and make it the focus of your attention.

Save that for your successes. Notice all the things you do well. Focus on the progress you make. Be aware of the positive impact you have on other people. Celebrate the obstacles you overcome.

Keep a digital, or written, record of all of these events. This helps the perspective shift stick. You want to reach the point where setbacks and failures can no longer derail you. Of course, you'll still feel the initial sting but the negativity doesn't stay with you. Half an hour or an hour later, you're back to focusing on what you want to achieve and where your next success is coming from.

Remember, you have a choice about how you see yourself and what you focus on. The truth is what you decide it to be.

How to bounce back from lost years and regrets

You may have recovered from a major illness and be struggling to come to terms with all it took. Perhaps you're in your 40s or 50s, completely disillusioned with your job and wondering to what purpose you've been working for the last 30 years? You might have just experienced a failed marriage, or long-term relationship, and be wondering how you could have invested so much into something that has now come to an end.

If any of the above has, or does, apply then there's something I want you to know. You *can* turn your life around. None of the above-mentioned events have to affect you beyond the initial emotional turmoil they generate.

This might be weeks, or it might be months. Grief and sadness are very natural and you're not seeking to remove them from your experience. What you cannot allow, though, is for these feelings to become permanent states that change your personality and outlook.

To ensure this doesn't happen, there's an important step you must take. At some point, when you feel ready, you must draw a line under the negative experience. You can no longer look back and say, "If only I'd done this instead," or imagine that things could have been different.

Remember, you can't get the "lost days" back. No matter how much you rue a missed opportunity, wish that things could have been different or think about the past, you can't go back and change those events. They're gone. Thinking about them only draws your energy away from making your present life as great as possible. Therefore, at some point, you must let go.

Letting go simply means ceasing to think about your regrets and mistakes. So, the next time you're wishing you never met your ex-partner, or did something different in the relationship, break the pattern. It might feel hard but tell yourself to, "let go."

Do it as often as you must. It might be 10 times a day, it might be 100. Eventually, the emotional vortex won't have such a strong hold over your thinking. As a result, you'll begin to see your life more clearly.

At this point, introduce your mind to a substitute thought. Instead of racking your brains over what might have been, channel *all* of your focus towards getting the most out of life, *right now*. Whenever a regretful thought or disappointing memory occurs, tell yourself, "that's why I must make the most of my life today." No more watching TV or browsing the internet when it's time to work on your dream. No more giving into doubt and fear when making important decisions. No more repeating mistakes. The pain of the past reminds you of the preciousness of today.

You might be wondering whether the same advice applies to the most devastating of life experiences. If so, learn from the example of Rubin "Hurricane" Carter.

The misfortune this man (whose story was popularised in the 2000 film, *Hurricane*, starring Denzel Washington) experienced was monumental. In and out of juvenile reform since the age of 11, he was falsely convicted of murder in 1967.

He subsequently served 19 years in prison for a crime *he did not commit*. At the time, he had a promising career as a boxer and was in contention for the middleweight championship of the world. However, when he was framed for the murder of three people in a bar, all his dreams were destroyed.

He launched many appeals against this false conviction, only to have them rejected. As the years passed, his case seemed helpless. However, hope arrived in the form of some benevolent Canadian property investors who made it their mission to help with his case after being moved by his story.

A lengthy court battle ensued, the upshot of which was that Carter had his conviction overturned and was finally released in 1985. Was he broken by this ordeal? Despite being separated from his wife and children, having a promising career as a middleweight boxer terminated and enduring the horrors of 19 years in prison, he displayed an amazing ability to make the most of his life once free. He remarried and became executive director of The Association in Defence of the Wrongly Convicted. A quote, before his death in 2014, should give you faith that, no matter how wasted, or tragic, your past may have been, a life of happiness is always possible,

> In my own years on this planet . . . I've lived in hell for the first 49 years, and have been in heaven for the past 28 years.[27]

There is nothing chaining you to your past. It exists only in your mind. As soon as you *focus on have a great time,* and making the most of your life, *now,* everything will change.

What to do if you're worried about getting old or how you look

A few years ago, I was reading an online article about some of the famous celebrities who'd undergone cosmetic surgery. A few of them were considered amongst the most beautiful people in the world. However, they weren't happy with both their appearance and the ageing process.

Often, the results of the surgery weren't pretty. They spoiled their natural beauty and turned themselves into a grotesque caricature. In doing so, they completely missed the point of life.

At present, we don't possess the technology to halt the aging process. As much as you may dislike the effects (and I do too), there's little you can do. Sure, you can exercise regularly, eat well, get plenty of sleep, limit the amount of time you spend in the sun and eliminate stress. However, ultimately, you're fighting a losing battle.

Nature is both your master and teacher. It informs you that your objective shouldn't be trying to look young forever or achieving a certain standard of beauty. Instead, the grey hair and wrinkles are a reminder that life is finite.

So, when you notice yourself getting older, or have never been happy with the way you look, what can you do?

Change your focus. Instead of directing your attention towards all the ways you're getting older, or the areas you don't like, switch it to *living as much as you can* while you still have life.

The occasional grey hair I notice is a reminder that I need to get the most out of my life *right now*. This spurs me on. It forces me to focus on my passions. As a result, I start enjoying myself more and, ironically, am no longer aware of my imperfections.

Remember, focusing too heavily on your appearance, worrying about ageing or thinking you're unattractive, will only bring your energy, and enjoyment of life, down. Ironically, you might *speed up* the ageing process through stress and worry.

Of course, there's nothing wrong with taking pride in your appearance and maintaining your looks. Just don't miss the point. You're here to *live*, not worry about how you look.

PART 3: CREATING THE LIFE YOU WANT

Everything you have learned, up until this point, has been preparing you for this moment. Now is the time to take the knowledge you've acquired, the strength you've gained and the skills you've developed, both through reading this book and facing challenges on your own journey, and use them to change both your world for the better.

Joseph Campbell wrote about this moment in his analogy of the hero's journey. After his lengthy research into mythology, he surmised that every individual wanting to do something significant with their life, will experience a journey of 12 different stages. For ease of understanding, he chunked these up into three major groups.

The first involves breaking free from the world you used to know. It's likely that a yearning for something greater, or different, led you to this book. Perhaps you've always felt there's something wrong with reality.

As your mind has developed, and you've learned and grown, there came a point where you rejected the world you were presented with and sought something greater. Of course, in doing this, you faced challenges. Friends, family, and society at large, attempted to keep you confined to the role they felt befitting of your background and talents. However, in resisting their pressure, you proved yourself worthy of passing into the second stage.

Here, you underwent a series of challenges that served as training to prepare you for the final stage of your journey. While some of these were physical, and some mental, they all served one purpose – to change your consciousness and beliefs. As a result, you emerged from your training with a new perception of reality and your capabilities. You became a limitless thinker.

With this attribute, you are now ready for the final stage. In Joseph Campbell's analogy of the hero's journey, this is called The Return. Having been brave enough to break free, and determined enough to develop new skills, you can't now go into hiding. Instead, you must venture back into the world from which you came and create some kind of change.

This is the challenge you face right now. You are ready to create the life you want. However, before you complete this final stage of your journey, there are more practical lessons to learn and wisdom to acquire.

To start with, you might be curious to know whether there are any financial constraints that might prevent your advance. How much money do you need to support yourself, and create a long enough runway, so that you can successfully launch a new product or passion?

And, what about time? How many hours will you need to set aside each week to create this new life?

Undoubtedly, you'll need to achieve results. Will this happen randomly, will luck just open the door? It's unlikely. Therefore, you must learn how to target your efforts, whose advice you should listen to and the mental approach you must adopt.

If you're creating a product, or selling your skills, it's likely that, in some capacity, you'll have to promote what you're offering. Must you have a large advertising budget to do this successfully? And, if you don't, what other methods are available to market your work?

These questions must be answered because you'll need to find a way to get noticed. You must stand out and, for some people, the thought of doing so provokes anxiety around the potential for ridicule and rejection. How will you cope with this?

Finally, The Return will continue to test your resolve. Other people will criticise you, it's likely that, in some capacity, your heart will get broken and you might even consider giving up. The strength and wisdom you display in handling these moments will determine whether, ultimately, you'll be successful.

A lot is riding on this final stage of your journey. However, you *are* ready. Read on to discover the final pieces of the puzzle and take your place among the other greats who get to live life on their own terms.

CHAPTER 9: ADVICE FOR WHEN BEGINNING YOUR JOURNEY

If you have a dream to be, or do, something with your life then my best advice is to jump, headfirst, straight in. Nothing can stop you. All the fears you have about going broke, or being ridiculed when you screw up, or friends distancing themselves from you, are illusions. I repeat, your fears are not real.

You will fail, though, many many times. However, you will also learn, grow, get smarter and stronger.

Enjoy the journey but also focus on the destination. There's no point putting conditions on your happiness (I'll only be happy when etc.). Instead, revel in every small step and battle won. However, you must also keep your eyes on the prize.

Be clear about what you're working towards. Use your imagination to feel how amazing it will be to get to this destination. With an exceptional work ethic, correct use of your natural talents, the ability to adapt to circumstances and a belief in your abilities or product, you will one day get there.

Why hope and desire are enough to get you started on your journey to a greater life

A few years ago, I watched the *Star Wars* film, *Rogue One*. Although far from a classic, there was one line that caught my attention. Delivered by Jyn Erso, it informs us that we don't need to have a plan, strategy or resources, to begin our journey.

Prior to this scene, Jyn has been introduced to the audience as a new recruit to the rebel cause. She's precocious, gifted and brave. However, as she discusses the future with her comrades, all seems lost.

Some of the more experienced Generals among the rebels are suggesting that it might be time to give up. The Empire has just unveiled their new planet destroying weapon (The Death Star) and is threatening to eradicate their home. Faced with such might, the Generals claim the rebellion is a lost cause and they should, instead, focus on their survival.

At this point, Jyn interjects. While she acknowledges that their situation is bleak (no concrete plans, no data they can use and no sign that they'll be successful), she points out that they still have one factor in their favour - Hope. Rebellions, she says, are built on this quality and, at least to begin with, it's enough.

As soon as I heard this line, I recognised that it rang true with my own experiences. For me, the "evil empire" was the system and my mission was to free myself from its influence. However, when I first embarked on this quest, aged 22, there was nothing in my life to suggest I could be successful.

I had no exceptional talents or skills and no money of my own. Furthermore, I had no experience in the passions I'd identified as a possible vehicle for escaping the system. I'd have to learn my craft from scratch.

The one thing I did have, though, was hope. Although I felt trapped, I never gave up. I wasn't positive or optimistic but I did think that, somewhere in the realms of time and space, there must be a way out.

This attitude was enough to begin my journey. Yes, the going was painfully slow and I encountered far more dead ends than answers but, slowly, I began to piece together a plan to escape.

At present, you may find yourself in a similar situation to mine. If you do, the most important thing you can do is keep your hopes alive. Do not give up. Entertain the idea that, somewhere, there must be a solution to your problem.

Added to that, you must have a desire to reach the next level. Even if you don't know what this level looks like, strive for improvement, progress and success. There should be a fire burning inside you to soar higher than your present predicament. If you can keep this desire alive, changes will follow.

Another fictional character provides an insight into how this will occur. Although also a movie, it is to the book version of *Dr No* that we'll now turn our attention.

About three quarters of the way through the story, James Bond has been captured by Dr No. Not satisfied with executing him immediately (we all know that one's gonna come back to haunt him!), he decides to play games with Bond. First, he'll engage in a bout of mental sparring as they share dinner and then, for his amusement, he'll force Bond to run the gauntlet of death.

During the meal, as the conversation turns to Dr No's future plans, he offers a profound piece of wisdom. He shares with Bond his own views on success and how, at least to begin with, little more than desire is required. He says,

> "I can see you are also a man who knows what he wants. On this occasion your desires will be satisfied. Do you not find that it is generally so? When one wants a thing, one gets it? That is my experience."
> "The small things" [Bond's reply]
> "If you fail at the large things it means you have not large ambitions. Concentration, focus - that is all. The aptitudes come; the tools forge themselves. 'Give me a fulcrum and I will move the world' - but only if the desire to move the world is there."[28]

Perhaps these were author Ian Fleming's own musings on success. From working as a journalist, to becoming a best-selling author, he must have known that his achievements had a lot to do with how much he wanted it.

As Dr No explains, this starts the process. What follows, is the acquiring of all the tools, knowledge and strategy needed for the realisation of your desires.

This should go some way to reassuring you. Everyone has access to hope and desire. They are simply an attitude and a feeling. However, what everyone doesn't do, is nurture these qualities.

This is where you must separate yourself. Frequently entertain the possibility that your life can change. Make sure you're always hungry to grow. Put everything you have into the important endeavours you undertake. With time, this desire will reveal the practical elements needed to ensure your success.

Why you only need £57/$70 a day to pursue your dream

What's your dream? Maybe it's to write a book or start a blog. Perhaps it's to set up a business. Maybe you want to excel as a coach or become a sports star. Whatever it is, the question of how much money you need to support yourself (especially in the early stages), while pursuing this vision, must be addressed.

That's why I've created the chart below. My aim is to show you that following your dreams is more financially accessible than you may have thought.

To do this, I've taken five key living expenses and created a minimum estimate of how much you'll need in each category.

Before looking at the numbers, there are a couple of factors to consider. First, the country I've chosen for my model is the UK (where I live). You need to bear in mind that the cost of living here is high. Therefore, if you're from another part of the world, you may want to adjust these figures.

Second, if you're from outside what's considered a "western" or "developed" nation then, unfortunately, these figures may not be of much use. However, using the five categories chosen, you should be able to calculate your own figures and apply them to your situation.

Remember, the point is to discover the *minimum* amount of money you need. Also, please bear in mind that the figures are based on a single person without children.

Expenses	Costs (per month)
Accommodation (including bills)	£700
Food (including meal out/take away/social drinking)	£400
Travel (non-vacation related)	£200
Social/Hobbies	£100
One Off Payments (Car Repairs/Clothes/TV) and Phone Bill	£150
Subtotal =	£1,550

Plus, if you were making this amount, you would be paying approx. £150 per month in income tax
Total figure = £1,700 ÷ **30 days** = £57

Before we look at the implications of these figures, there are a few points I must explain. As I've already mentioned, these figures are a minimum. There's no room for luxury. Instead, it's about the essentials.

With the accommodation category, spending £700 a month is unlikely to provide you with a home of your own. In fact, renting a place on your own might also be beyond your reach. Instead, you might have to seek a flat share or roommate. So long as your accommodation provides a roof over your head, a bed to sleep in and an internet connection, this is enough.

Of course, you could choose to live with your parents. Understandably, though, you may feel you've outgrown this living arrangement and that, a place of your own, is a necessity. However, if you're comfortable living with your parents and they're comfortable with your plans, then why not save yourself a substantial expense?

Note that my breakdown is £57 every single day. That means seven days a week. Of course, you don't have to work seven days a week so it might be easier to think of earning £400 per week. This could be done over five days, or less, or more. The choice is yours.

Also be aware that this is an approximate, ball park figure. It's unlikely to be completely accurate to your situation (even if you're living in the UK). The exact figure isn't what's important. The idea of earning, and living on, less, to free up time to work on your dream is what you should take away from the chart.

Note that my breakdown hasn't factored in any money for a vacation. I classify this as a luxury, not a necessity. Of course, if you're of a mind that it's the latter, then you might be able to put £5 a day into a holiday fund. However, as with all the expenses in this chart, you shouldn't lose sight of the bigger picture.

Seth Godin once said, "Instead of wondering when your next vacation is, you ought to set up a life you don't need to escape from." What's going to bring you more joy? A couple of weeks escape from a mundane life or a lifetime spent doing the things you love? Surely, having to sacrifice vacations for a few years to achieve this is worth it?

The purpose of calculating the £57 a day figure is to show you that financial concerns shouldn't stop you from pursuing your dreams. Almost anybody living in a G8 country could earn the approximately £21,000 (£57 a day over the course of a year) needed to put themselves in the race (The UK average salary, combining both full-time and part-time work, currently stands at just over £29,000).[29] However, what are the implications of living on just £57 a day?

To start with, you can no longer be a consumer. Designer clothes, or maybe even new clothes, have to go. Perhaps your gym membership has to follow. Working out at home, or in the park, will suffice. New cars can no longer be afforded. Whatever gets you from A to B will have to do.

Of course, there's no *real* loss in being unable to afford these luxuries. You'll still be perfectly healthy and your ability to enjoy life will remain undiminished. However, there can be a *perceived* loss.

You might feel less of a person. Perhaps you'll feel you're worth more than £21,000 a year and that, when compared to what your friends or peers are earning, this figure is embarrassing. Maybe you'll feel you're missing out when people you know are heading off on vacations, buying their own homes or regularly enjoying nights out.

If you experience any of these symptoms, then adopt a long-term perspective. While your friends may be getting "system rich" (wealthy by society's standards but never wealthy enough to be financially free), you're giving yourself the opportunity to be truly rich.

This means wealth in both experience and money. By giving yourself the time needed to create the life you want, you're imbuing your days with a new sense of purpose and adventure. While your friends work mainly for money, and have to deal with the stress and boredom that comes with it, you're working for the love of what you're doing or creating and, as a result, get to experience the inspiration and personal reward this brings.

Furthermore, one day, you might have the chance to be financially free. Salaried jobs rarely offer this opportunity. First, there's the heavy tax demands. Second, the whole nature of the job is to make someone else rich.

Make a living through your dream, though, and the sky's the limit. There's no salary cap. Your company might grow to the point where it's worth millions and you're the sole, or majority, owner.

Who are the richest people in the world? The ones that followed their passion. We're inspired by the Elon Musk's and Steve Jobs's of this world. The faceless chief executives who've worked, and wormed, their way to the top of the corporate ladder don't interest us.

To join the ranks of the people who make a living from their passion, discipline will be required. For example, look at my suggested monthly food (and drink) spend - £400. To meet this limit, you might need to shop at a cheaper supermarket. You might also need to buy in bulk and then make a large evening meal which can be used for two or three lunches on the following days.

This discipline will also affect your ability to socialise. Perhaps you'll have to limit alcohol infused nights out to only two a month instead of every weekend. Would the prospect of cutting back in this fashion make you feel like you're missing out?

If so, remember that everyone has the ability to adapt. Perhaps you can invite friends over more regularly. Maybe you can find social activities that don't come with such a hefty price tag.

This might even be a great time to revaluate your social circle. Are there people you're socialising with just for the sake of having something to do? If there was an emergency, would these people be there for you? If not, maybe now is the time to cut them out of your life. Less people equal less distractions, less money spent and more time to focus on creating the life you want.

Don't worry, though, you'll still be able to enjoy your life. There's no cap on meeting genuine friends and engaging in the hobbies you love. You'll just have to plan ahead. Be aware of your budget, know your financial limits and work within these boundaries. If you reach the point where you're running low for one month, then spend more time working on your passion or project. The expenses will be minimal and you get to do something you find rewarding.

Furthermore, when it comes to your finances, you might not have to drop as low as earning £21,000 a year. Perhaps you're currently on £100,000 a year. However, in earning this amount, you have to give an average of 50 to 60 hours a week to your job.

Could you find a role with less hours, go part time, or work as a consultant? With one of these options, perhaps you would earn half of what you did before - £50,000. This is still a substantial income, plus you have the added benefit of 20 extra hours a week to work on creating the life you want.

I wouldn't want you to misunderstand the purpose of the £57 a day chart. You don't have to just make £21,000 a year. This figure was chosen, primarily, to demonstrate that the need to make money is no obstacle to pursuing your dreams.

Regardless of the country you reside, you should be able to make a basic amount to live on. Once you've done that, you can dedicate all of, or as much time as you want, to grander ambitions.

Of course, if it's within your capabilities to earn more than £21,000 a year while still having time to commit to a more meaningful project, then do so. Just be aware of how you spend your time. One of the problems of well-paid, employed jobs, is that they place substantial demands on your life. If you're working for 50 hours a week, commuting for 10, and require another 10 for household chores and other activities, that doesn't leave you with much free time to focus on anything else.

The £21,000 figure also gives you an amount to aim for. If your new business or project is earning you this minimal sum, then you know it's enough to live on. With this knowledge, you could potentially cease all other forms of money-making activity and throw yourself into your new project full-time (thereby giving yourself the option to make more money).

Whatever option you choose, avoid being chained to society's rules. Sometimes less is more. A richer life can be gained through the pleasure of working on a project you love rather than being paid well but feeling like you're trapped.

With this in mind, reassess your current financial situation. Take a look at your expenses and see if there are ways you can cut back. Remember, your value isn't determined by what you own. It's determined by what you do, create and how you treat other people.

How much T.I.M.E should you invest in your project or business each week?

The 10,000-hour rule was popularised by Malcolm Gladwell in his book, *Outliers*. It's based on a study conducted over 40 years ago by scientists Herbert Simon and William Chase. They investigated how long it took to become a Grandmaster in chess, discovering that there were few overnight successes. In fact, their research indicated that it took on average 10 years, or 10,000 hours, of practise to become an expert or Grandmaster.

After this discovery, similar research was undertaken in other fields like learning a musical instrument and sports. The studies all seemed to draw the same conclusion - to be outstanding at anything, you'll need to put in 10,000 hours of practise.

This figure has important implications for you. No matter what your dream may be, there seems little way of getting around the fact you're going to have to spend a lot of time perfecting your craft, building your audience and spreading your message.

Of course, the 10,000 rule is not set in stone but it does provide a useful indicator of the time commitment needed. For greater applicability, break it down into years, weeks and, finally, days. You might want to remember this acronym (T.I.M.E).

The 10,000-hour rule
Indicates a
Minimum of 2 hours 45 minutes
Every day

That equals 20 hours a week and 1000 hours a year. Bear in mind that the 2 hours 45 minutes figure is *every* day (weekends included). Of course, you may not work weekends and this is fine. So long as you get your 20 hours completed each week, or 1000 hours over the course of a year, it doesn't matter when you do it.

How do you compare? Take a moment to figure out exactly how much time you're consistently giving to creating the life you want. It may not be as easy as calculating how long you spend practising a sport or developing your artistic ability. It might mean hours spent researching a project, promoting your work on social media or taking extra tuition to learn a new skill.

Whatever it is, write the figure down. Is it close to an average of 2 hours 45 minutes each day?

If not, you're probably in the majority. After 10 years of working in the personal development industry, speaking to people about their dreams and listening to some brilliant ideas, most people have one factor in common. They don't dedicate enough time to creating the life they want. When I ask them about the number of hours they put in, the answer is usually the same, "Oh, a bit at the weekend if I can. I've just been so busy with work lately that I've had the shelve the idea for a while. I'll get around to it at some point."

In my early days of trying to become a best-selling author, I was the same. It was easy to tell myself I needed to earn an extra bit of money (through tennis coaching or hypnotherapy) or that I'd been working hard and needed to relax. Ironically, I'd then get frustrated with my lack of progress. "I just need the right contacts, or a lucky break like an influencer sharing my work," I'd tell myself. Or, I'd look at someone more successful than me and wonder, "what do they know about generating book sales that I don't?"

There was no secret, or shortcut, though. In fact, the answer was pretty boring. I needed to put in the hours so I could write more books, make more contacts and learn enough about marketing so that I could promote myself effectively. Without scheduling the time, and having the discipline to sit down and do it, nothing was going to change.

Where will *you* find the time? You could go the burn out route and do it when you return from work (assuming you have no kids and are single). Or, it might be easier (and you'll be fresher) if you wake up an hour earlier and get an hour's work done before you go to your day job. Either way, perhaps you can get close to completing 10 hours between Monday and Friday. Then, forgoing some of your weekend activities, you complete another 10 hours on Saturday and Sunday.

Another option is working less hours at your day job. Scale back. Can you negotiate with your boss and go down to 30 hours, or 4 days, a week? If that won't work, the least you could do is stop working overtime. Even better, if you have a skill you can use on a freelance basis, then perhaps you can quit your job and work independently. With the greater control over your time this brings, it then becomes easier to find the 20 hours a week needed to work on creating the life you want.

Finally, if you have enough money, you could quit your job and live off your savings while you work full time on your dream. This would give you more than the 20 hours a week needed to make progress with your dream. In fact, you should be able to achieve 40 or 50. This would, potentially, halve the time it takes for you to be successful.

Whatever you choose, remember *you* are in charge of your life and, through that, your time. The busyness epidemic that most of us experience is self-imposed. You don't *have* to work 50 plus hours a week at a job you don't enjoy. There are alternatives.

Finally, remember that everyone is busy. We all have the same 24 hours. Just make sure you're busy building your dream rather than conforming to society's notion of how you should live your life.

Why you have a 66% chance of achieving your dreams

Have you ever been inspired by the idea of doing something amazing with your life? Perhaps almost everyone, at some point in their life, has. However, a lot of these dreams fade as we become adults and face the so called reality of making a living, having a family and providing for our future.

Why do we allow this to happen?

Yes, on the surface, our commitments take over but there's also a deeper issue. We fear failure.

What's the main message you hear when it comes pursuing your dreams? "Go for it, put everything you've got into your work, and there's a good chance you'll be successful." Or, "Be careful, only a tiny percentage of people who pursue their dreams ever succeed?"

Depending on your age at the time, the latter message may come from parents, teachers, careers advisers, work colleagues and even friends and partners. When it's repeated again and again, and also reinforced by the media, your dreams of doing something extraordinary with your life end up looking ridiculous. "Who am I to even think I could achieve something so outrageous?" you'll ask yourself as you consign your dreams to the scrapheap.

And that's how it happens. A negative message is repeated again and again until eventually accepted. This then creates a limiting belief which prevents any form of action. Rational beings that we are, we'll play it safe and accept a mediocre life over something that could lead to disaster and only carries with it a minuscule chance of success.

You might recognise this way of thinking. Perhaps you've fallen into this trap in the past and prematurely given up on your dreams. If so, what if I was to tell you that, rather than the 1% chance of being successful that society gives you, your chances for success are actually a generous 66%? Would you back yourself on these odds?

Before committing to your dream, you'll probably want to know how I arrived at this figure. After much analysis of the people who are both successful, and fail, at living their dreams, I realised they can be broken down into four categories.

While most people fall into the first three, and fail, the reasons for doing so can easily be avoided. You, with the knowledge of how the journey to realising your dreams works, will give yourself a much greater chance of ending up in the fourth category and being successful.

Before looking at our first category, it's worth mentioning that the following analysis applies to any dream. You might want to become a pro footballer, make a living selling oil paintings or cookery books. Irrespective of the competition you face, the four categories will remain the same.

Also, for the sake of the explanation, we're going to assume you have 1000 people sharing the same dream and competing against you. Obviously, depending on the nature of your dream, there may be more, or less. For example, if you want to become a pro footballer, you might be competing with 10 million other teenagers, and young adults, who share the same dream. This may sound like far too much competition. However, you must remember that, when lots of people desire a position, there are usually more of them available (for example, FIFA statistics indicate there are 65,000 professional footballers in the world).[30]

Let's explore the four categories now and see why your chances for success are a lot greater than you may have thought.

1. The Procrastinators

The first thing you can do with your 1000 competitors is to eliminate 900 of them. These are the people that talk a great game but never deliver. They won't pick up a phone, they won't sign up to a course and they won't buy any kit. Sure, they're inspired by the idea of living their dreams but they won't take any concrete steps to make them happen.

A lack of discipline and courage is what stops a Procrastinator. They'd rather their dream was handed to them. Of course, this will never happen and this is why you don't need to worry about them stealing your spot.

2. The Triers

Once you eliminate The Procrastinators, you're left with only 100 other competitors. Although these people are a level up, they're still not your direct competition.

A trier will pursue their dream for a year, possibly two. They will invest in their idea, putting both time and money into the endeavour. On the surface, it'll look like they're serious. However, underneath it, they lack the right mindset.

A trier's approach to living their dreams is one of testing the water. They'll dip their toe into this new world, keen to see what it's about, but quickly retreat when feeling out of their depth.

The problem is that they're unable to reject their conditioning. The system tells them that 9/10 new businesses fail, or that their dream is impossible to achieve, and they believe it. Therefore, when they face their first major adversity, it's likely they'll quit.

Instead of understanding it as an opportunity to learn, grow and get stronger, they'll see it as proof of what they've already been told. Dreams don't come true unless you're born with an exceptional talent or blessed with good luck.

For this reason, you don't need to worry about the Triers taking your spot. They may be ahead of you in the early stages but, unless they reject the system's conditioning, it's guaranteed that they'll give up at some point.

3. Minor Players

This leaves you with only 20 other competitors. These people are exceptional. They're all highly motivated, willing to take action and don't view failure as an end point. As a result, they all enjoy some form of success.

To a degree, they're able to monetize their passion. For the pro-footballer, they might get signed to a lower division team which, although pays a salary, isn't quite enough to live on. The artist might get their oil paintings feated in a gallery. The cook book author might fail to get a major publishing deal but self-publish their book and build a small following instead. All of them, to some extent, are living their dreams. However, what stops them from making the full-time transition?

The short answer is that they're not crazy enough. They're not willing to risk it all. Every person pursuing their dream will face adversity. It hits hard, and regularly, and there's only so much a sane person can take. Before long, even a Minor Player will start to ask questions about the impact that the pursuit of their dream is having on the rest of their life? Is it keeping them away from their family for too long? How long can they keep living on a minimal amount of money? How many years is it going to take?

When they stop liking the answers to these questions, they'll quit. Having already attained a modicum of success, they'll tell themselves they'll revisit their dream when circumstances permit. However, as there is never a "right time" to do anything, they'll continue waiting while dealing with the day-to-day commitments of the new life that has now replaced their once glorious dreams.

Furthermore, they're not ready to invest *everything* in their dream. They have a plan B. They're still influenced by societal conditioning, believing that the factors determining their success, to some degree, lie outside of themselves. As a result, they make other plans just in case they fail.

Of course, this seems sensible. However, in doing so, they don't commit all their resources to their dream, nor experience the increased focus that putting everything on the line can bring.

With competition for places being so hot, just a small decrease in your focus can cause you to lose out to a more committed competitor. As a result, you can eliminate 17 of the Minor Players. After 2 to 10 years of pursuing their dream, they'll give up.

So, what does it take to reach the very top?

4. The Dream Achievers

You are now faced with only 3 other competitors for the title of Dream Achiever. All of you have something in common. If it comes down to it, you're prepared to die for your dream. That's what separated you from the 997 other people all wanting your spot. You're not going to stop working *until you're successful* and no consequence is going to scare you into turning back. If you become homeless, then so be it. If you lose friends and family, then as heart-breaking as it is, you'll continue. Nothing will stop you unless your heart ceases to beat.

This determination, combined with a belief in yourself and your product, and the ability to adapt to circumstances, is what turns you into a dream achiever. However, despite the qualities listed above, your place is still not assured.

I promised you a 66% chance of success. You are still facing two other competitors just as skilful and hungry as you. With both of them looking to claim your spot, does this reduce your chances of success to 33%?

No. People with a scarcity mindset overlook an important fact. You don't have to be the best to live your dreams. In football, there's Messi and Ronaldo. In cookery, there's Gordon Ramsey and Jamie Oliver. In the soft drink industry, there's Coca Cola and Pepsi. There's room for more than one person or brand at, or close to, the top.

You only have to fill one of these positions. Sure, it would be nice to be number one, but is it completely necessary?

Of course, you might still be concerned there's a 33% chance you'll fail. How do you handle that?

If it was to occur then, once again, you'll need to approach your failure with a sense of perspective. If you got this far – to the final stages of being a Dream Achiever – it's likely you'll have experienced significant successes along your journey. These still count. The character you've gained in overcoming virtually all obstacles is still inside you. Furthermore, it's likely you've made some money, gained contacts or achieved victories that are likely to impress people in other industries. Can you now tweak, or reassess your dream, in such a way that you still get to do something you enjoy even if it wasn't what you originally intended?

For example, perhaps you had your heart set on being a professional football player. Sadly, you failed in your attempt. Can you now take everything you learned from that journey and become a football coach?

Once you've adjusted to this new idea, perhaps you set your sites on coaching one of the top teams in your country. Maybe it isn't as fun as playing, but it gives you a greater sense of fulfilment. Ultimately, once you've achieved your new dream, the disappointment from the past will no longer matter.

Hopefully this breakdown has given you some encouragement. Now, you understand that much of being successful at achieving your dream is down to persistence. Sure, you're going to have to adapt, and perhaps adapt the nature of your dream but, if you just keep going, something amazing will happen - almost all of your competitors will drop out. Furthermore, you don't even have to be the best to achieve your dream. You just need to be good enough.

The key takeaway of this analysis is that you should never underestimate the power of taking a little bit of action towards the realization of your dream - It puts you ahead of nine tenths of the competition!

Of course, this doesn't guarantee success but acting on your dream gives you the opportunity to learn, grow and increase your confidence. It's worth taking a risk. Your chances for success are greater than you think and, even if you were to fail, you will only emerge from the experience a stronger and wiser person.

Why your intuition can provide reliable life guidance

What is your intuition? The National Science Foundation estimates that we have between 12,000 and 60,000 thoughts every day.[31] How do you decipher between the mundane and the divine?

The first thing to know is that intuition is not *directed* thought. For example, as part of a routine, you might spend time each day visualising yourself being successful. When you do this, you run different scenarios through your mind and focus on clear outcomes.

This is directed thought. You're fixing your mind on a specific objective with the intention of programming your subconscious to provide ideas for your goal's achievement. Doing so requires effort and focused attention, two qualities never associated with intuition.

The next thing to know is that your intuition is not your worries and fears. To varying degrees, everyone experiences negative thoughts. You might be one of the few who have trained their mind to such an extent that they're rare. Or, they could be a feature of your daily life. Even worse, perhaps they've taken over.

Negative thoughts are rarely rooted in reality. As French philosopher Michel De Montaigne once said, "My life has been filled with terrible misfortunes, most of which never happened." Robert Leahy's book, *The Worry Cure*, reveals that 85% of our worries never materialise. This research sends a clear message that your worries are to be ignored. They don't carry any useful information and will only drain you and cause you to procrastinate.

Random thoughts are another type of thinking that shouldn't be mistaken as intuition. These can occur at any time of day and are, seemingly, unconnected to your situation or point of focus (for example, you could be in a classroom learning and suddenly you find yourself thinking about what you watched on Netflix last night or anticipating what you might eat for dinner this evening).

However, upon closer inspection, random thoughts are usually connected to something you've been doing earlier in the day or week, or something in your environment that's reminded you of a task that needs completing (for example, while scrolling through the contact list on your phone, you're reminded to give a friend a call). Such occurrences reveal that random thoughts have more to do with your memory than a higher dimension.

Now that we've eliminated the three other types of thought (Directed, Worries and Random), you are left with your intuition. Don't expect it to strike frequently. In fact, you may even go weeks or months without hearing its call.

When it does strike, though, it will be accompanied by powerful and positive emotions (joy and excitement being primary amongst them). Such feelings let you know you've found an answer or that something important has been revealed.

You then have a choice. Do you act upon what your intuition reveals or do you dismiss its insight as impractical and something that would never work in "the real world?" (more on this in a moment).

Your intuition might provide you with an insight on a variety of subjects. It could be something relatively small such as a title for a blog post or a slogan for a marketing campaign. At other times, it might advise you on a major life decision or provide confirmation that you're on the right path.

In Joseph Murphy's book, *The Power of Your Subconscious Mind*, he recounts the story of Professor Louis Agassiz, from Harvard University, whose intuition revealed to him the missing part of a fossil.

Agassiz was a naturalist who lived during the nineteenth century. For two weeks, he struggles to decipher and classify the dimensions of a fossilised fish. Eventually, making no progress at all, he set his work aside and took a break from the project. That very evening, and the one after, he had vivid dreams that revealed the correct dimensions of the fish.

The first night he had the dream, he couldn't recall the image upon waking. However, the next evening, he remembered to keep a pencil and paper by his bedside so he could capture the vision in the middle of the night.

Incredibly, upon visiting the lab the next day, he discovered the sketch he made in the night was accurate. After chiselling away the superfluous rock, as instructed by his night time sketch, the image of the fossilised fish was revealed. His intuition had shown him the way.

Oftentimes, throughout my journey, I've heard the call of my intuition. One of the most memorable occasions was at the start of 2017.

Five years into my quest to become a best-selling author, I attended a personal development event in London. I'd spoken at this event 6 months prior and, after my talk, a woman had bought a copy of my book, *Escape The System*.

It just so happened that she was in the audience again and, after the talk had finished (I wasn't speaking this time), she came up to me and struck up a conversation. Much to my delight, she told me she'd read *Escape The System* and loved it. So much so, it had contributed to her decision to move countries and pursue a new job.

Although far from the first time I'd received positive feedback on my work, the conversation had a profound impact. I was left with the feeling I *would* achieve my long-held goal of becoming a million selling personal development author. It was a *certainty*. So long as I continued to do the work, I'd get there. Therefore, no matter what was happening in my life - the length of time it took, being conscious of getting older, potential money difficulties - I *had* to stay focused on my goal and keep going.

This is just one example of my intuition. I've had similar experiences regarding relationships and discovering my life purpose.

My intuition also reveals titles for books, subjects for talks and ideas for videos. On each occasion, whether my intuition reveals a major or minor insight, the experience *happens to me,* rather than me creating it. The message is usually very clear and communicated through *a knowing* or emotion (I don't hear voices).

In attempting to activate your own intuition, the first thing you need to know is that it can't be forced. Control won't work. Instead, you must use the clues left by other people's experiences.

In my case, I noticed that my intuition usually struck after a period of time engaged in intense thought upon a subject. For example, I could be working away on a blog post, having already selected a title, and then I'd take a break. While taking a break, and washing the dishes or brushing my teeth, suddenly, a more captivating title for the blog post would flash through my mind.

I didn't force this experience. Instead, my mind was still "whirring away" on the subject, half consciously, half drifting while I was semi-engaged with the physical activity.

Something similar occurred in the example of Professor Agassiz. Although his intuition spoke to him while he was in a completely unconscious state, the tell-tale signs of intense conscious focus were there. During the day, uncovering the hidden dimensions of the fossilised fish was all that he thought about. As a result, when he relaxed and took his focus away from the subject he was working on, his intuition struck.

You should be able to replicate this formula. Set aside periods of time for both intensely focusing on what you want to achieve and relaxing. You'll find that once you've charged your mind with enough energy, it will respond when you least expect. Just make sure you're able to write down, or remember, the insight it reveals.

Can you trust your intuition? Will it guide you to the life of your dreams or lead you to take crazy risks that end in disaster? This question is especially important when you consider the possibility that your intuition might prompt you to pursue a course of action that challenges society's notions of what's possible or acceptable. For example, should I listen to my intuition when it tells me *I can* become a million selling author? What if I fail and, as a result, miss out on the chance to have a semi content life raising a family and working a regular job?

What about you? Should you be listening to your intuition when it tells you to quit your job and launch your new business? Or, should you listen to your intuition when it tells you to make a potentially risky investment in a particular stock or cryptocurrency? In my experience, the answer is "yes."

Throughout our lives, we are given little reliable guidance. Our parents, as well-meaning as they are, tend to advise us on how to become copies of themselves. Either that, or, they're so afraid of us getting harmed, their guidance is overly cautious.

Following the crowd won't work either. This will, at best, lead to a life of security and comfort. At worst, it could lead to inner conflict caused by ignoring your true self. Either way, a self-actualised will be out of reach as you spend the majority of your days conforming to society's expectations.

Can you trust authority figures? Doctors, the media, government, corporations, teachers and religious leaders will all offer insights on how to live your life. On the surface, they appear to know what they're talking about. Afterall, these people, and institutions, are revered as the most intelligent amongst us. Furthermore, the position of power they've attained gives them a level of credibility that is almost undeniable. However, is it wise to listen to them in every situation?

It's not the remit of this book to explore conspiracy theories. However, one thing that the investigation of authority figures does reveal is that appearances are deceiving.

While they may claim the advice they offer is with your best interests at heart, most of the time, they are only serving themselves. A psychiatrist has a professional (and sometimes financial) incentive in diagnosing you with a disorder and prescribing medication (even when there are known, harmful side-effects). Corporations need you to buy their products, even when they have zero impact on your quality of life, to keep making a profit. The media needs you to keep paying attention, even when they're not reporting the truth, to stay relevant. Sometimes, these are hidden motives behind the guidance authority figures offer and, for this reason, anything they say should be treated with suspicion.

So, where does this leave you? With few credible external sources that can be relied upon for guidance, you must look within.

What have you got to lose? As highlighted above, listening to your parents, following the crowd or obeying authority, will, most likely, lead to an incomplete life. Therefore, as crazy as it may sound, you must learn to trust your inner voice.

Sometimes, doing so, can feel like the riskiest decision of all. Who are you to say your beliefs and intuitions carry more weight than conventional wisdom? Persist with this line of thinking and you'll discover that your intuition can be surprisingly reliable.

Research undertaken at Boston College, and published in *The Journal of Organizational Behaviour and Human Decision Process* in 2012, indicates intuition can be just as effective as an analytical approach when it comes to decision making. In fact, depending on the expertise of the decision maker, sometimes it can be even more effective. The report states,

> Testing intuition against analysis, Pratt and co-authors Erik Dane of Rice University and Kevin W. Rockmann, of George Mason, found that people can trust their gut and rely on intuition when making a broad evaluation - one that doesn't include a subset of additional decisions - in an area where they have an in-depth knowledge of the subject.[32]

This research is fascinating. It appears your intuition is at its most effective, "when making a broad evaluation." This relates to our topic because what are major life decisions if not broad evaluations? You either decide to stay in your present job or quit and pursue your passion. You either decide to marry your boyfriend or girlfriend or call an end to the relationship and look for someone else. There's no "subset of additional decisions" to be made.

This is why you can trust your intuition with important life decisions. When there isn't a large amount of data to analyse, it won't get confused. It knows your heart's deepest desires and will keep you on a path aligned with their realisation.

When following your intuition, don't be disappointed if it fails to deliver a winning insight every time. You might be feeling inspired about the new idea for a lesson you want to teach, or a talk you want to give, only to find that it's met with a lukewarm response.

This isn't a reason to turn your back on your intuition. Over a long enough time scale, it will deliver, and the times when you think it's misfired, are usually valuable experiences that can be used to assist your progress at a later date.

Finally, don't be discouraged by the difficult path, or decision, that your intuition may prompt you to take. Just because something is right doesn't mean it will be easy. You could face all kinds of challenges as a result of following your intuition but this shouldn't stop you from listening to it. Remember, failing to act on your intuition comes with its own set of consequences that could prove insurmountable years, or decades, down the line when you finally face them.

CHAPTER 10: ESSENTIAL KNOWLEDGE FOR ACHIEVING RESULTS

As valuable as learning theory and experiencing spiritual breakthroughs can be, does there come a point in your life when you need to produce some kind of result to move forwards? Perhaps you want to see an increase in the sales of your products. Maybe, you want to step on the scales and see a reduction in the number of kilos or pounds. Perhaps, after time spent working on your social and dating skills, you want to see a new boyfriend or girlfriend in your life. Maybe you're determined to enjoy a greater success rate with your clients. There are numerous ways to measure your progress and all of them provide *real* evidence of your development. However, achieving them can be harder than you imagine as there are key skills and attributes you must learn.

One of them, and perhaps the most important, is a focused mind. Your thoughts must be occupied with your objective, rather than the hundreds of other distractions that can derail you during your working day.

Hard work is also important but hard work, without knowing whether your work is effective, won't be enough. Furthermore, a certain level of detachment is needed to achieve results. Excessively worry, or become desperate to succeed, and it's likely this emotion will scare off the people and breakthroughs necessary for success to occur.

Achieving results is a process and you will improve with time. Read on to discover how and start making a dent in the goals that are important to you.

Why you must become obsessed with your most important goal

There's a dark side to the subject of success and personal development. It's not all positivity, love and light. Almost without exception, creating the life you want requires incredible commitment and back breaking hard work.

More than this, though, is the level of focus you must bring to your endeavour. Only an obsessed mind will bring forth the creations and reveal the insights needed to succeed. The thought of what you want to do, or become, has to dominate your mind.

In the U.K, we have a £50 note as a means of currency exchange. On the back of this note, is a picture of James Watt, the 18th century Scottish inventor whose improvements to the steam engine helped bring about The Industrial Revolution. Underneath his picture is a quote which reads, "I can think of nothing else but this machine."

These words reveal what it takes to achieve your most important goals. Morning, noon and night, Watt probably entertained a mental image of the machine in his mind. Furthermore, to anyone that would listen, he probably talked about it constantly. He was so engrossed with the thought of improving the steam engine that little else registered.

You must reach a similar stage. Your subconscious responds to your habitual thinking. Keep your mind focused on what you want to achieve and it will respond with answers, innovations, a direction to follow and the chance encounters that will bring about success.

This is why having an obsessed mind is so important. Most people drift through life on auto pilot. They read the newspapers, watch TV, endlessly surf the internet and gossip with friends. In short, they have distracted minds.

You, however, with your desire to create, or do, something amazing, must have a focused mind. Think about what you want to achieve on your journey to work, think about it while you're changing, bathing and washing the dishes and think about it in between sets when you're working out.

Furthermore, limit the amount of time you spend watching TV or Netflix, browsing the internet, social media and listening to the radio or podcasts. These are all vital moments that could be used to focus on your goal and, thereby, increase the speed by which you achieve it.

Jonny Wilkinson used the power of obsession to turn himself into, arguably, England's greatest rugby player. The following story, from The Times newspaper (on the 22nd May 2014 - after he announced his retirement), highlights the lengths he'd go to ensure his game was at the level it needed to be.

Phil Larder, England's defence coach, recalls a training session where the team had to practice a tackling drill. Jonny only made eight tackles out of ten and was dissatisfied with his performance. Even though they were flying out to the Rugby World Cup (in 2003) the next day, he made Larder wake up 10 of the other players at 5.30am, 4 hours before the flight, so that he could perfect his tackling. They repeated the drill and this time he scored ten out of ten.

Someone else who used the power of obsession to reach the top of his field is chef, Rene Redzepi. Head chef of Noma, a restaurant in Copenhagen voted the best in the world by Restaurant magazine in 2010, 2011, 2012 and 2014; Rene was so obsessed with culinary perfection that he worked 10,000 hours in just 3 years.

By his own admission, he is consumed by his work. In an interview with The Sunday Times Magazine, he reported that,

> I work all the time. I don't even count the hours now but it's somewhere around 98 a week. For the first 5 years of my career, I was so submerged in my work that I couldn't think of anything else. I had no clue what was going on in the news.[33]

Of course, you may feel this level of obsession verges on being unhealthy. This is understandable. People succeed without working 98 hours a week. However, nobody succeeds without some degree of focus.

Finding a balance is a skill you'll have to master. Be aware, though, that your goal needs to consume you, to some degree, for you to achieve it. This isn't a bad thing. Without people who are prepared to let their goals become obsessions, there would be little progress or change.

Take it easy on yourself when trying to make progress

Look at my speed dial below. The information I want you to focus on is the 23mph AVG. This is the average speed I travel at.

Before a weekend break in 2016, it read 22mph (I gained a mile per hour over the course of the two days).

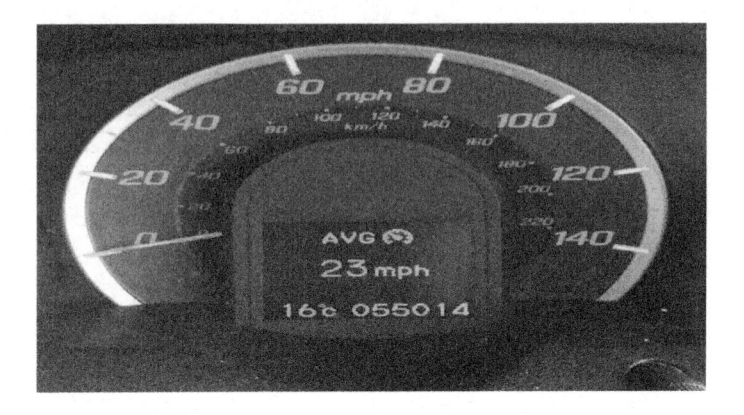

On that particular weekend, I had an anniversary break with my girlfriend. We travelled to the Cotswold's (a roundtrip of about 200 miles), using many of Britain's motorways and travelling at speeds occasionally in excess of 80mph. However, over 5 hours of travel only adjusted my average speed by 1 mph. How could such high-speeds have so little impact on my overall average?

The answer is revealed in the figure below the 23mph. Not the temperature, but the 55,014 miles I've travelled in this car. It forces you to think about the long-term trend rather than a short-term spike.

Many people get disappointed when, after a week of being productive, motivated and working solidly on their dream, very little changes. They might make some progress, but the sum total of their effort doesn't really take them any further than when they started. Disheartened, they're tempted to give up.

What they don't realise, though, is that they're combating a lifetime of driving between 10 and 20 mph. So what if they race around at 80mph for 3 days? How can they expect this sudden spike to drastically alter the course of their lives when it's not consistent with the years prior?

My speed dial serves as a reminder of how long it can take for your life to progress if you've only recently changed your habits or given a full-time commitment to a project. Be understanding with yourself. Progress can, sometimes, take time.

It took single-celled organisms 600 million years to evolve after the Earth was first formed. It took them a further 2.75 billion years to evolve again and develop into multi-cellular organisms (plants and animals). The process of evolution and change is a slow one and necessarily so because, if you get it right, you never go back to where you were before.

Bear this in mind the next time you're frustrated by the seemingly pedestrian rate at which you're progressing. Perhaps you're looking for the wrong thing. Instead of immediate results, be happy with laying the foundations for permanent change.

Although not as appealing, perhaps this outcome will serve you better. Afterall, something gained quickly can also be lost at a similar speed. However, if you know exactly why you advanced, and the steps needed to get there, then you have a formula you can repeat again and again.

Therefore, perhaps increasing your speed by 5 mph every month will be more effective than increasing it by 50 mph over a weekend and then being unable to sustain your momentum. Aim to be consistent rather than fast.

Why you must target your efforts

Pareto's Law states that 20% of your efforts will yield 80% of your results. Furthermore, 80% of your time is set to be, somewhat, wasted as it will only produce 20% of your outcomes. While the percentages can change (sometimes it will be 90/10 or 70/30), the principle behind Pareto's Law is surprisingly accurate.

How many people have you ever been out on a date with? Including the ones that never led to a second encounter, let's say the figure is between 30 and 50. How many of those dates led to a relationship that lasted a lifetime or produced children? Most likely, only one or, perhaps, two.

Have you ever made a lot of money on a property deal? Upon doing so, did you look back and realise that in the 50 or so hours you spent looking at the house, purchasing it and then selling it (including all the legal work at both ends), you earned more money than in 2000 hours spent working at your job?

If you run a business, have you ever taken time to calculate which of your customers bring your highest returns? You might be surprised to find that only a select few (roughly 20%), prop up the rest of your business.

Pareto's Law teaches you that there's a non-lineal relationship between your efforts and results. The key take home is that you shouldn't delude yourself into thinking that, just because you're working hard, you're being effective.

With this knowledge, scrutinise your current work and figure out what is making an impact and what is barely justifying your time. Be ruthless. Perhaps you currently spend 8 hours a week on social media. You feel you have to, as many marketing experts have told you about the importance of this medium.

However, when you run your analytics, you discover that very few people, from the varying social media platforms, ever visit your website and become a member or subscriber.

What do you do? Continue to listen to the experts, or heed Pareto's Law and cut back (or cut out) the time you spend on social media?

This decision might be made easier when you discover that the one 'in-person event' you attend each month, generates, on average, a paying client every two months. What if you were to increase the time investment from 3 hours a month, to 10, by attending more events?

My own investigation revealed some surprising results. Over the course of the 8 years that I've been blogging, I've written over 60 blog posts. Just one of them, *Self-Improvement is Masturbation: Tyler Durden's 3 Rules for an Exciting Life*, has generated more traffic and sign ups to my website, than the other 59 combined. What's the lesson?

Clearly, I need to produce more Tyler Durden or *Fight Club* related content. This might apply to books, videos and talks, as well as blog posts.

Can you see how this works? Look at all areas of your life and discover where the results are coming from. Then, regardless of whether this accounts for only 20% of the work you do, start eliminating parts of the 80% that are unproductive.

As mentioned earlier, ruthlessness is the key. You must fight your conditioning. It's likely you've been raised to believe that hard work pays off. Therefore, you just have to put the hours in, regardless of what you're working on, and, eventually, you'll see results.

While this approach may, ultimately, work, why wait 10 years when you could apply Pareto's Law and achieve your goal in 3? You just have to get comfortable with the idea that, presently, some of the work you do is without merit. Therefore, cut back drastically, or stop doing it.

This applies to all areas of your life. How much time are you currently wasting doing exercise routines that bring little results, maintaining relationships that add nothing to your life or watching television you don't actually enjoy? Take a complete Pareto's Law inventory and you might find that, without making any sacrifices, you free up a lot of time for the work, people and hobbies you love. All it requires is a different way of looking at the world.

Why you shouldn't let expert advice stop you from experimenting with your own ideas

Whether you are employed, self-employed or an entrepreneur, there'll be a recognised way of operating, and being successful, in your particular field. Furthermore, this doesn't just apply to work. You might be learning a new sport or hobby and your coach or online tutor tells you that it must be played in a certain way. Or, perhaps you're a new parent and the books you've bought, and the classes you attend, tell you your children must be raised according to some tried and tested rules. Should you always follow their advice even when you know it isn't going to work?

Muhammad Ali is recognised as the greatest heavyweight boxer of all time and yet, he rarely listened to the experts. He liked to do things his way. Boxing writer, Hugh McIlvanney, noted that,

> He made it hard to distinguish between amateurishness and creative originality, and his immunity to convention helped him to expand the tactical inventiveness in which he took huge pride. He rightly believed he understood his fighting equipment better than anybody else and he prosecuted the belief with an unbreakable resolution that was as crucial to his success as any of his physical attributes.[34]

This is interesting. Here we have a man who reached the pinnacle of his profession yet was "immune to convention." He didn't keep a high guard to block his opponents blows, he leaned back to avoid punches (a big no no) and he threw punches while on the move instead of setting himself to gain extra power. All of these techniques fly in the face of boxing's best practises. However, Ali still became one of the greatest boxers in history. How is this possible if expert advice is as valuable as we're led to believe?

When I first began working as a tennis coach, there was a set way we were supposed to deliver a group lesson. This always, without fail, started with a 5 or 10 minute physical warm up. With younger children, between the ages of 4 to 7, this might also involve another 10 minutes of co-ordination-based training.

While doing my training, I didn't question this lesson plan. However, once I qualified and began teaching my own classes, I quickly realised that following this formula wasn't going to work.

The main problem was a lack of time. Most of the children I taught attended only one class a week. This mean that, if I followed the guidelines, out of an hour-long session, they would only be playing the sport for 45 minutes (we were also trained to do a 5-minute warm down and debrief at the end of the session). This was a problem. The parents were paying for their children to learn a new skill. They didn't want to look over and see the kids running around without a racket in their hand.

Furthermore, the children found the warm ups boring. They'd come to play tennis, not run around a court or partake in some other form of exercise. Plus, I knew that the children didn't need to be warmed up. Their enthusiastic sprint from the car to the tennis court indicated that they were ready to play. So, what was I to do?

I didn't take me long to drop the physical warm up. Instead of instructing them to do laps, they could either begin by rallying gently in the service boxes or we'd do some other tennis related warm up game. I wasn't going to watch my classes dwindle because I'd been told by my governing body that there was some "correct" way to teach a tennis lesson.

The result? Happy kids and well attended classes.

What can you take from this, and Ali's, example? Should you disregard all expert information?

No. Sometimes the experts in your industry have useful insights. However, this doesn't mean you should follow them to the letter.

There should always be room for experimenting with your own ideas. Perhaps you have a better way of doing things than someone who has no idea about the specific nuances of your situation or personality. There's certainly no harm in experimenting. Your guiding principle should be "follow results, not the appearance of knowledge."

Why you shouldn't give a damn about being successful, even with your most important projects

Have you ever found yourself working so hard to achieve something but, regardless of your effort, you still can't succeed? It's almost as if the more you want something, the more it eludes you.

If so, you might be getting caught in the "effort trap." Victor Frankl talks about this in his bestselling book, *Man's Search For Meaning*. He explains that,

> Again and again I therefore admonish my students both in Europe and in America: Don't aim at success - the more you aim at it and make it a target, the more you are going to miss it. For success, like happiness, cannot be pursued; it must ensue, and it only does so as the unintended side-effect of one's dedication to a cause greater than oneself or as the by-product of one's surrender to a person other than oneself. Happiness must happen, and the same holds for success: you have to let it happen by not caring about it. I want you to listen to what your conscience commands you to do and go on to carry it out to the best of your knowledge. Then you will live to see that in the long run - in the long run, I say! - success will follow you precisely because you had forgotten to think of it.[35]

The key point from this passage, as pertains to being successful, is "not caring about it." Of course, you want to succeed, and all your efforts are geared towards this aim. However, you don't worry about outcomes or fear you might fail.

By adopting such an attitude, you're actually displaying belief in your success. Afterall, would a seasoned business person constantly fret over sales and check their numbers on an hourly basis? No, he or she would be confident that everything will be on track and only check at the appropriate time. It's this relaxed attitude that removes all the unconscious factors that can sabotage your success.

This also rings true when it comes to forming romantic relationships. You may have gone years without a date but you can't approach the task of finding love from this position. If you do, the desperation will be evident in your voice and actions. Instead of being relaxed, you might come across as intense and scare the other person off. In the end, you cared so much that it backfired.

Of course, it's understandable, whether your goal is business or love, that you care. Everybody does. However, there's a difference between caring and being confident and caring and being desperate.

If you fall into the latter category, begin to detach from the outcome you care so much about. As Frankl advises, "listen to your conscience" and carry out its promptings without any thought of outcome.

Adopting this attitude generates a confidence that can't help but attract success. People and companies will react to you as if you're an expert. And, without even appearing to try, the outcomes you desire will enter into your life.

CHAPTER 11: PRACTICAL TIPS AND STRATEGIES FOR GETTING YOUR WORK NOTICED (AND MORE)

It's all too easy, and alluring, to think that, once you've created a product or developed your skills to a sufficient level, your journey is over. What you have created will sell itself and, all you have to do, is sit back and reap the rewards.

Perhaps success works this way for a tiny minority. However, what if you find that you've expended an enormous amount of energy in the creation phase, but your journey is far from over? Must you now confront the reality that you'll need to work just as hard, or even harder, at getting your work noticed?

In the likely event that this is the case, an important question should now be at the forefront of your mind. How are you going to make paying customers or clients aware that you, or your product, exits?

Conventional wisdom dictates that you'll need to advertise. You must pay to place your product in prominent places likely to gain your target markets attention. However, how do you ensure you're not wasting your money and is the role of advertising still as relevant in our social media driven age?

Exploring this question may lead you to seek other methods to promote your work. Perhaps you'll take an organic approach, using your existing network as a platform to launch yourself to a wider audience. Maybe you'll become adept at using email marketing, constantly delivering value to your subscribers by providing great offers, or free content, so they're primed to purchase when you have something to sell.

Whatever approach you take, you must learn how to make yourself, and your product, stand out. In the process, you might have to overcome a personal hurdle. Perhaps you want to remain in the background and let your work speak for you.

How will you overcome this tendency to avoid attention? Furthermore, how will you cope if you face criticism when you step out of your comfort zone? Read on to discover the answer to these questions and more.

Why advertising might be a waste of your money and what to do instead

Over nearly 20 years of being self-employed, I've run three different businesses (tennis coaching, hypnotherapy and book writing and selling). During this time, I've been responsible for generating my own work and clients.

This was difficult, and daunting, at first. I had no marketing experience and, often, was taking a stab in the dark when it came to promoting myself. I assumed that I'd need to advertise as that's what everyone else seemed to do. As a result, I invested in different advertising services in the hope it would generate the clients and customers I required.

Unfortunately, in most cases, it didn't. Across the board, my experiences with advertising have been disappointing.

Fortunately, I was wise enough not to throw too much money at the different campaigns I attempted. However, whatever I did spend, was usually wasted.

Despite my many failures, though, I have generated a substantial amount of business over the years that I've been self-employed. Something must have worked. In trying to understand what that was, my mind went back to when I first started working as a tennis coach in 2003.

My first move in this industry was to ally myself with a local tennis coaching company. The owner had two tennis clubs, multiple schools and a sports centre as part of his empire. My job was to teach the hours he couldn't and he paid me a cut of the takings (I started on a measly £12 per hour). As a result, I didn't have to do a lot of advertising. I received my work through him but had to accept I'd be paid a lot less because I was piggybacking off his name.

Although it has its downside, this strategy was effective. Why do all the hard work yourself? Why not cut out all the trial and error and potentially wasted advertising revenue and, instead, go straight to where your clients or customers are?

In answering that question, you might point to the lower financial returns of getting your work through someone more established in your industry. It's true that I probably ended up earning less than 50% of what I could have *potentially* made. However, this was potential. There was no guarantee I'd have been able to generate the business myself.

In 2011, I struck out on my own. I secured my own tennis courts and almost all my clients wanted to continue with me. This meant that, initially, I didn't have to do much advertising. It was a case of "porting over" rather than starting anew.

However, now I had to rely on myself when it came to acquiring new clients.

I did this when advertising my holiday camps. Between 2000 and 5000 (depending on the length of the holidays) A5 flyers were designed and printed and then delivered to local schools. Often, I'd have to pay a £10 to £40 distribution fee to the school bursary and they would insert them in the children's book bags.

This strategy worked. Every Summer I would see new children and, upon asking where they found out about the camps, they'd reply via the flyer. My outgoings weren't even that great. I'd spend about £150 on flyer design and printing and an additional £100 on greasing the schools so they'd hand the flyers out. Over the course of the holidays (especially the longer summer ones), these flyers would probably make me about £500 in *new* attendees. However, this says nothing of the repeat business that over half of these children would then go on to generate.

I began working as a hypnotherapist in 2005. One of the strategies I used in an attempt to gain clients was adding my name to online hypnotherapy registers. These were usually free to join (so long as you had proof of your qualification and affiliation to one of the governing bodies) and they promoted your services to the local area. I also paid to promote myself on Yell.com, experimented with Google AdWords and paid for an advert in a local magazine.

None of these strategies generated much business. Ironically, the best return came from the least amount of money spent (the online registers). Disgruntled, I decided to implement the same strategy I used for my tennis coaching.

The first clinic I started working at was only 20 meters from where I lived. Serendipity had placed it there and the owner was wonderfully accommodating and fair on price. However, the downside to this clinic was that it was very small and had no receptionist.

As a result, it didn't generate any new business. I would always bring the client to the clinic, rather than the clinic bringing clients to me. It was nothing more than a convenient base.

Refusing to give up on a tactic that worked for my tennis coaching (partnering up with a more recognised individual, or organisation, and using their profile to create awareness for my work), I visited two other clinics in neighbouring towns. Both were larger, with multiple rooms and a greater footfall. They also possessed something I discovered would be key to growing my hypnotherapy business - talkative receptionists.

As a general rule, people frequenting complementary health clinics are open to the idea of alternative therapies. They don't have limiting beliefs about treatments being too unscientific. Therefore, when client X comes in for her weekly massage and chats to the friendly receptionist about needing to give up smoking, she's open to the suggestion of booking a session with the clinic's new hypnotherapist.

This is what I benefitted from when I began working at these two new clinics. Although their rates (room hire) were far higher than my first clinic, they generated enough new business to warrant the increase. In fact, this approach quadrupled my clients in the space of six months.

By 2008, I began scaling back my efforts to attract new hypnotherapy clients. I needed time to write my first book.

However, in 2015, after redesigning my hypnotherapy website, I launched a new advertising campaign.

Again, this was inspired by the success of doing leaflet drops for my tennis coaching business. At a cost of approximately £400; I had flyers designed, printed and then delivered to the catchment area for my local clinic. This campaign ended up paying for itself. It brought me in a total of three new clients, some taking more than one session and, therefore, covering my costs and earning a small profit on top.

I became a paid author in 2012. However, because of my previous experiences with advertising, I was loathed to spend money promoting my book.

Instead, I relied almost entirely on free marketing. One of my key strategies was building an email list. I'd offer the potential subscriber, in return for their email address, a free eBook (at a later date, I changed this to a free course) when they signed up to my website.

As I nurtured this list, providing them with free content in the form of blog posts and videos, I would also make them aware of my books. I rewrote my first book, *Screw The System*, in 2015, and changed the title to *Escape The System*. It was then relaunched at the start of 2016. I made sure to promote it to my email list, offering them a discount if they bought it within the first five days of the launch.

I repeated the same formula with my second book, *How to Create an Income Without Working a Boring Job*, in 2018. In both cases, I considered the campaigns a success. Approximately 2% to 3% of my list bought a book.

Alongside email marketing, I've also given a number of talks across various personal development groups in London. After presenting these talks, I'd promote my book, offering a discount to anyone purchasing on the day. Typically, purchase rates were between 5% - 25% of the audience. However, these are relatively small audiences, with a maximum of 60 people attending.

The final book selling strategy I deployed was of my own creation. I happened upon it by chance. Using connections made on social media, *I would simply tell people about my book and suggest they bought it.*

This wasn't spamming. I vetted the people I approached. Before I mentioned my book, I had to see that they'd shown an interest in themes similar to the ones I write about (For example, they'd mentioned, on their own posts or in the comment section of mine, how they hated the influence of the system and were looking for ways to break free). Then, I'd simply comment on their post, or send them a private message, and suggest they might be interested in reading my book. Roughly 75% of people would then make a purchase.

I also used this strategy to acquire 1 to 1 tennis coaching clients. When I first began tennis coaching, I only taught group lessons (where most of the money went to the coach I was working with). Therefore, to increase my income, I needed 1-to-1 clients.

To gain these, I simply asked parents if they wanted to invest in 1 to 1 coaching for their child. Again, this wasn't spamming. I *only* asked the parents of children who were showing potential in their group lessons.

With this proviso, it was almost a no brainer. Their son or daughter was doing well in their lessons, enjoyed the sport and the parents were keen to push them further. If they had the money, it was almost certain they'd then sign up for 1-to-1 coaching.

The final and, to date, only, successful *paid* advertising strategy I've used has been Amazon Ads. I've been using them to boost the sales of my first book, *Escape The System*. So far, the results have been, largely, positive, with some weeks seeing me 10x my sales.

My strategy for Amazon Ads has been fairly simple. Advertising and key word research is out of my comfort zone so I don't want to spend months researching only to find that I was still screwing it up. It was easier to pay two friends who were also authors, and experiencing success with Amazon Ads, to tutor me on how to launch successful campaigns. With only three hours of these coaching sessions, I was able to set up rudimentary campaigns that enhanced my sales.

Despite this increase in sales, it must be mentioned that my profits have been minimal. I'm making less per copy sold than before and, in the case of Amazon US, my campaigns are running at a loss. Of course, there's an argument that the increased sales might lead to readers buying future books, signing up for coaching and attending my events, but it's still too early to gauge whether this is true.

Overall, my experience with Amazon ads has been positive, and the potential is clear, but I still have a lot to learn about making the campaigns consistently profitable. However, in my 17-year history of being self-employed, this has been the *only* paid advertising that has been worth the investment.

Facebook Ads, which I experimented with in 2017, were a waste of money. I used them to promote a free course I'd created. My hope was that people would sign up to my website (and I'd capture their email addresses) in return for receiving the course. Despite having spent a significant amount of money hiring someone to film and edit the video I used for the Ad, and putting hundreds of pounds into the advertising budget, I hardly saw any return. Deeply frustrated, I haven't used Facebook Ads since.

Before I conclude my advertising and marketing story, it would be remiss of me if I neglected to mention one of the most effective strategies I've experienced when it comes to generating new business – word of mouth. Currently, I spend less than £500 a year advertising my tennis coaching and hypnotherapy businesses. This may sound like a miniscule budget but I don't need to spend anymore. Word of mouth and recommendations do the rest.

I can't keep track of the amount of times that parents have approached, or called, saying a friend's child has enjoyed their lessons with me and now, their son or daughter wants to join. Word of mouth has been less prevalent with my hypnotherapy clients (possibly because the treatment is of a more personal nature and, therefore, people are less inclined to discuss their issues with friends or acquaintances), but I've still experienced many clients mention they've discovered me through a friend who used my services.

It's harder to gauge the impact of word of mouth on my book sales. Of the few thousand books I've sold, I've probably only had personal, or email, contact, with a few hundred readers. Their communication is, typically, very positive and I have had readers buy multiple copies of my books to gift to their families, or clients, and some tell me they've recommended my book to friends. This seems to suggest that word of mouth still plays an important role with my book sales but, without exact figures, it's hard to say.

Clearly, word of mouth is a form of marketing that is win-win. Extra clients at no extra cost. However, how applicable is it to a new business owner, and how do you go about developing it?

I found it very hard to generate word of mouth during the infancy of my businesses. This was for two reasons. First, there was a lack of clients or readers to talk about my products or services. If you only teach 20 children a week, or have 3 clients on your entire hypnotherapy roster or have only sold 50 copies of your book, then there just aren't the numbers needed to benefit from word of mouth. It took me a few years, in each business, before I started to experience this phenomenon.

The second reason it took me a while to generate word of mouth was that, initially, the services I was offering (especially the tennis coaching and hypnotherapy), were not as exceptional as they could have been. Like virtually everyone who's new to a line of work, I was a rookie. Despite my training, I still had a lot to learn and needed to build my confidence.

Once that happened, though, word of mouth grew and I've been relying on it ever since. It has been the most effective form of marketing for me. However, because it takes time to build, and other strategies also have their merits, here's a summary of my 17 years' worth of experience.

- My *general* rule is that paid advertising is a waste of money, especially paying for adverts in magazines or newspapers, paying to be on Yell.com or the Yellow pages and paying to be featured on a digital advertising screens in petrol stations or shops. Of course, the advertisers are going to tell you how effective it is, what great returns they deliver and how you'd be crazy to miss out, but don't be fooled by this (especially if they've contacted you first).

- Personal experience would lead me to place Facebook and Google Ads in the above category. However, I've known people who've experienced great results using these platforms.

  My lack of success probably reflects more on me than any fault with the system. However, my failings do indicate that it's unlikely you'll experience success with Google or Facebook Ads unless you spend a lot of time, and possibly money, learning how to use them. Be prepared to put in many hours of research on how to run an effective campaign and understand that you might lose some money before you see a return.

- Leaflet or flyer drops have been good to me. At a minimum, I've made my money back. At best, they've consistently delivered a profit.

- Finding an individual, or organisation, with a larger audience than you, and partnering with them to generate clients, is a sound strategy. Just be prepared to give up a large percentage of the money you could make for the privilege of doing so.

- Asking people if they want to buy your product, or service, works. Afterall, if you've created something that will benefit their lives, they'll want to know about it. Therefore, don't be shy. If the relevant conversation comes up, tell them about what you do. Don't spam them though.

  Also, recognise there's a limit to the amount of 1 to 1 communication you can do. It's time consuming.

- Email marketing works. Always look to build your list and never hesitate to tell your audience about a new product launch. However, bear in mind that to make the most of email marketing, you'll need a large number of subscribers, possibly into the tens of thousands.

Why you should use your existing network to sell your new product

When I launched my first book, back in 2012, numerous people advised me to use my existing network to boost my sales. After having spent nine years working as a self-employed tennis coaching and hypnotherapist, I probably had a database of well over one thousand people that, at some point, I'd worked with. This was a warmish audience who might have been interested in my book (or just helping me).

Unfortunately, I was too afraid to ask. I'd developed a limiting belief that my tennis coaching and hypnotherapy clients wouldn't understand, or accept, me as an author who'd written a book called, *Screw The System*. I was their friendly tennis coach or hypnotherapist. It would cause cognitive dissonance to now present myself as a rebellious author.

My other problem was that I didn't know how to promote my book. As much as I believed in it, and had spent countless hours perfecting it, I drew a blank whenever people asked me what it was about. I felt like an idiot whenever answering their questions, and was certain that my lack of articulate "elevator pitch" was making the book sound very unappealing. As a result, I tried to avoid conversations about what I had written and quickly changed the subject if anyone asked about my book.

Clearly, this was a terrible strategy. The outcome of this avoidance, and launching with no audience to sell to, was that it took me 6 weeks to sell a copy of my book outside my immediate family. It was a further 14 months before I reached 100 sales.

Nobody knew about the book. I was blaming Amazon when really, I should have been blaming myself for not tackling my limiting beliefs and using the ready-made audience I already had.

Hindsight offers me the ability to look back and see how things could have been different. If I could have my time again, then I'd have developed an email list from all of my past and present tennis and hypnotherapy clients. Of the over 1000 people I'd worked with, plus friends, family and acquaintances, perhaps a few hundred might have signed up.

Using this list as a platform, I could have emailed them prior to the launch and told them about the book and what to expect. When it came to launching, another email could have been sent, offering a discounted price on the book for a limited time only. This would have, possibly, led to 50 or so sales, a couple of positive reviews and, potentially, some recognition with a wider audience. Momentum would have been generated and, perhaps, a platform created that would have led to greater sales.

I know this because, with my second book, I executed that plan. The results were as explained above (although the numbers were greater as, this time, I had an email list of 1300 people).

Emboldened by this success, I sent out a separate email campaign to my tennis coaching and hypnotherapy clients letting them know about my work as an author. This was 6 years after the launch of my first book but I was still keen to see the reaction. I wanted to learn the truth about the cognitive dissonance I had previously feared (and, perhaps, generate a few extra book sales).

Since I never had a structure email list for all the tennis and hypnotherapy clients I'd worked with, the job was time consuming. I searched through old addresses on my accounts and added these to a more readily available my current clients. As a result of the scattered nature of the email addresses, I only ended up messaging approximately 500 people out of a potential 1500. The results were interesting.

A grand total of two people complained about spam. Many more, although by no means a substantial number, either bought the book or wished me well. The vast majority, just ignored the email and didn't reply.

This outcome confirmed that my limiting belief was completely misplaced. By and large, people don't care. You are not going to damage your standing with your current and long-time clients, your reputation at work or your relationships with friends and family, by going in a different direction and releasing a new product or offering a new service.

Most people will just shrug their shoulders, maybe wish you well, and then get on with their own lives. Some will support you and possibly even invest in what you're doing. A very small minority might be critical. However, any negativity they level at you won't have any lasting impact.

It's important to realise that the fears you have about launching a new product, and moving in a different direction, have no basis in reality. Although the awkward nature of announcing a different facet of your personality to the world is understandably uncomfortable, there is nothing to fear. In fact, by using your existing network, you have a lot to gain.

When I finally did announce my book writing endeavours to my tennis and hypnotherapy clients (6 years later), I was surprised by some of the people who supported what I was doing. I'd made assumptions that certain individuals weren't going to understand and, possibly, think twice about continuing to use my services as a tennis coach or hypnotherapist. Ironically, a few of these people were the ones who bought a copy or spoke to me in person and expressed an interest.

This taught me that I should never make an assumption about how someone will react to a new product or project. The limiting beliefs you carry around in your mind only cloud your judgement. Furthermore, they are yours alone, often not shared by anyone else.

For these reasons, you should consider using your existing network to help promote and support any new endeavour you launch. They are the ones who are going to add the credibility and social proof needed to draw in a wider audience. Ask them to write reviews or tell their friends about what you're doing. Some of them may even have contacts in your industry.

Remember, there is nothing to fear when letting people know about your new project. In fact, doing so will help you grow personally and professional. Overcoming the anxiety around exiting your comfort zone will open you up to learning new skills. I only became relatively proficient at promoting my work by facing some uncomfortable moments where I didn't know what to say. The same process will happen for you. Your existing network is a starting point for you to practise these skills. Pass this test, and you'll be ready to promote to the world.

How to highlight the benefits of your product to your customers

The photo below is of the popular UK breakfast cereal called Weetabix. As with most cereals, it would be classified as a carbohydrate. However, if you take a look at the bottom left corner, you'll notice that Weetabix's marketing team are promoting the protein content of the cereal and claiming this is for "healthy muscles."

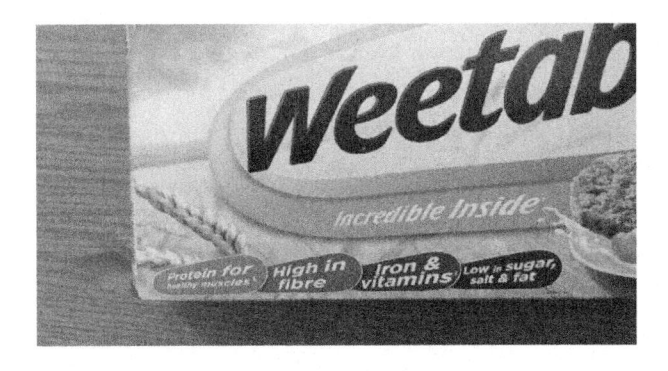

Weetabix never used to do this. I've eaten the cereal for well over 20 years and not once have they ever mentioned the protein content of their cereal. Furthermore, the amount of protein per block has always remained the same - a rather unspectacular 4.5g per serving. So, why are they promoting this now?

The short answer is that we've become a more protein conscious society. This applies to two important demographics.

First, are the bodybuilders, or frequent gym users. The popularity of weight training has increased massively since the turn of the century, picking up even more since 2010. Gyms are now packed with men, and increasingly women, keen to build a physique similar to their favourite Instagram or YouTube influencer.

Protein is the key ingredient in muscle building and every image conscious individual is hunting for sources. Therefore, if a company highlights the fact their food has a slightly above average amount of protein, compared to their rivals, then they could be claiming an important share of the market.

The second demographic are vegans. As with gym usage, veganism has also exploded in the last 10 years, with a 360% growth in people eating this way.[36] In a diet where all animal products are off limits, they must look for alternative sources to gain their protein.

For these reasons, I shouldn't have been surprised when I picked up the box. The product hasn't changed, but consumers desires have, and that's why Weetabix are marketing it differently.

Despite their slightly disingenuous claims (4.5 grams of protein per serving is pretty insignificant), it's a smart move. They're stressing the benefits of their cereal in a way that solves their customers problems.

This was something I learned about when studying how to promote my book. I paid for various Kindle coaching courses and also signed up to a membership with Fizzle (a website showing you how to build an online business). As a result of this learning, I started restructuring my content and marketing material.

Below, you can see the impact on the contents page of my first book. The updated version is in brackets, the original, without. Notice how I'm moving away from purely descriptive chapter headings to ones that let the reader know the benefits they'll receive from buying the book.

One: The Awakening

(The Awakening: Your Journey Begins)

Two: The System

(The System: What it is and how it holds you back)

Three: Finding The Path

(How to Find your Path through Life)

Four: A Guiding Light

(The Power of Having a Dream and How to Create One)

Five: Transforming Power of Belief

(Why your Beliefs Determine Everything)

Six: Belief in Action

(How to Use the Power of Belief)

Seven: Soul Power

(Soul Power: The Secret to your Happiness and Success)

Eight: The Skill of Detachment

(How to Rise Above your Present Environment)

Nine: Letting Go

(Why Controlling your Life doesn't Work and what you need to do Instead)

Ten: Releasing The Genie

(How to Connect with your Genius and Overcome Fears, Doubts and Negative Thinking)

Eleven: Overcoming Adversity

(How to Overcome Adversity)

Twelve: The Climb to Greatness

(How to Grow Stronger than The System)

Both mine, and the Weetabix example, should give you some idea of how to promote yourself and your work. Emphasise benefits, not features. Put yourself in the mind of your potential customer or client. What do they want to achieve through buying your product? Once you've identified this need, you can then present the solution in your promotional material.

Why you should consider setting a cap on the amount of TV you watch

How much TV do you watch each week? When calculating this figure, make sure to include Netflix, YouTube viewing, clips you might watch on Facebook or Instagram and any visits to the cinema. Furthermore, bear in mind that this figure might be higher than you think. The average UK citizen watches 27 hours of TV a week.[37]

Once you've got your number, ask yourself how much you can reduce it by? Is all the TV you're watching adding to your life? Does it inspire you? Are you learning from it? Or, are you just watching for the sake of it? Are you watching it because you can't face the mental or physical demands of working on your important projects?

I don't think there's anything wrong with watching TV (and remember, I include Netflix, YouTube and cinema under this definition). Film is a medium that has inspired me like few others. I've learned a lot from documentaries. Overall, TV has had a positive impact on my life. However, I do recognise its negative impact as both a form of brainwashing, and an avoidance strategy for hard work.

For these reasons, you should put a cap on the amount of TV you watch. If you currently watch 15 hours a week, then go down to 12. If you watch 10, reduce it to 8. Whatever your number, try to cut back by a few hours or more.

To make this practice truly impactful, *you must record how much TV you watch each day*. Either take a stop watch, or make a mental note of what you're watching, and then record it in a diary or on a database. This shouldn't be too difficult as movies will always have run times or you'll know that your favourite Netflix show has 50-minute episodes (or however long they last). It's harder to track your YouTube usage but, if you're diligent, you should still be able to figure it out. Add up the numbers each day and make sure you keep below your weekly cap.

Recording how much TV you're watching keeps you accountable. Two hours less (or whatever figure you're reducing by) TV viewing a week may not seem much, but it adds up to 104 hours a year. This is the equivalent of over two weeks' worth of work that you could shift over to a project you're passionate about. In a world where success depends on fine margins, this *does* make an impact.

Another practice you might want to adopt is reducing your monthly food spend by 20%. Do you know how much you spend on food a year? If you're looking to save money so you can work less hours at your day job and, thereby, free up time to work on your passion, you should.

It's hard to find a meaningful figure when it comes to discovering how much the average person spends on food. Lower income individuals and families tend to spend less but, what they do spend, equates to a greater percentage of their income than those with greater resources.

Whatever category you fall into, you should start to keep track of your food spend. After two or three months of doing this, you should have an accurate idea of what this will equate to over a year. Once you have this total, figure out what you will need to do to reduce it by 20%.

Reducing the number of takeaways, and meals in restaurants, is a great place to start. Cutting down by just two a week should make significant reductions.

Once you've done that, you might want to consider *increasing* the number of times you visit the supermarket each week. While this may sound counter intuitive, it actually decreases the amount of food you waste. Only make weekly, or bi monthly visits to the supermarket (or wherever you shop), and you might find that some of the food you buy is unnecessary and ends up going out of date. However, if you only buy for the next few days, and make use of the food you actually have, there's little chance of miscalculation.

Making large evening meals, and then eating the left overs for the next couple of lunches, is another great way to reduce your food bill. Another option is buying the products your supermarket currently has on special offer and then changing when those offers change.

Finally, you might want to cut down on the number of snacks you eat. Do you ever eat when you're not actually hungry? Perhaps you have chocolate, biscuits or cheese on toast, a couple of hours after your evening meal. End this habit. Hold out until you go to bed and then eat again in the morning.

Or, maybe you snack an hour before lunch. If so, drink some extra water, stave off the cravings and wait another hour. Cutting out the times when you're eating without feeling hungry will not only help you reduce your food spend by 20%; it will also assist you to lose weight and improve health.

The benefits of adopting this practice are far reaching. Work out how much you earn per hour. Then, calculate how much you are saving, over the course of a year, by cutting back your food spend by 20%. Divide this figure by how much you get paid per hour, and you'll have the number of hours you've saved over the course of a year.

Let's say it's 50 hours. That's 50 hours you don't have to work seeing freelance clients. Or, that's 50 hours of overtime you no longer have to do. That time can now be spent working towards creating the life you want, or in any other way you deem valuable.

The number one excuse people give, at the seminars I run and attend, on social media and in coaching sessions, for not being able to do the work they love, is a lack of time. With these two small changes (watching less TV and cutting back on your food spend), you could free up over 200 hours a year.

The time to build a new and meaningful life for yourself *does exist.* You just need to investigate the minutia of your life to discover where.

How to overcome the anxiety of sharing your work, project or business with the world

In a previous section, I mentioned the anxiety I experienced when first sharing my book, *Screw The System*. I told no one about the launch. Furthermore, I didn't want people to ask me about the book and tried to change the subject if the conversation headed in that direction.

This was all because I feared my work wouldn't be accepted. For 9 years, I'd presented myself as a friendly, 'nice guy' to clients and new acquaintances. Now, I was propagating, what some might consider, controversial views.

It wasn't just with my existing clients that I feared rejection. While promoting my work online, I was also concerned that I might attract criticism. Although these were people I didn't know, I feared they might rubbish my work or disagree with my views.

The negative impact of this fear has already been explained in a previous section. Now, the focus shifts to overcoming it. Perhaps you have your own creative vision. Maybe you have ambitions to become a YouTuber, write your own book or blog, create music, sell your art, or even start a new business. In launching this project, perhaps you fear that you'll become a target.

What's going to happen? Are people going to ridicule your efforts? Are they going to judge you? Are you going to fail and not a single person will be interested in your work? Or, might they even love what you do?

Your mind might present you with 101 different possibilities when you finally take the plunge. Furthermore, it will play tricks on you and come up with a bunch of crazy scenarios relating to your fears about what might happen.

If any of these thoughts occur, then the most important thing to remember is that they're perfectly natural. The next thing to know is that *they're not real*. They're just ideas in your head and bear no relevance to what may, or may not, happen.

You need to understand that, 99% of the time, and this even extends to friends and family, people are so wrapped up in what they're doing, they haven't got the energy to be negative about something you're doing. Own this knowledge because it gives you permission to be who you want to be, say what you want to say and do what you want to do. Create with freedom because the worst reaction you'll encounter is silence.

Even if you do receive criticism from someone you know, or an anonymous source, this can still be spun to your advantage. As long as the person isn't mudslinging (in which case you should disregard what they have to say), then they might be providing you with vital feedback. Have they got a point? Are they highlighting an area of your product or performance that could be improved? If so, how can you enhance your work?

It stings when you receive any kind of criticism (even the productive kind). However, once the emotion wears off, you can embrace the idea that challenges to your work are actually a good thing.

Another fear people have when sharing their work is failure. This strikes on two levels.

The first is the embarrassment of having to explain to friends, family, and anyone that asks, how you're doing when failing to make sales or gain clients. You may have, understandably, hyped your new business or product launch. 6 months later, when someone asks how it's going, and you have nothing positive to report, it can feel very uncomfortable. You might imagine them thinking, "I knew they didn't have what it takes to succeed."

Fear of failure can also occur over concerns about meeting your own expectations. It's more than likely you have a goal you're aiming to achieve (e.g., gaining 10,000 subscribers to your blog). What happens when you can't even get 10?

It can be crushing to see all your hard work come to nothing. You might count up all the hours you've spent on the project and feel you've wasted your time. Or, you might get angry at the world for not appreciating your creation or understanding your work. Even though you've gained 10 subscribers, you can only focus on the 9990 you failed to acquire.

If this situation applies to you, then you need to remember that you don't have to be perfect. Switch your focus. Stop thinking about what you haven't achieved, and start focusing on your accomplishments (no matter how small they are). Your final goal is important but, especially in the early stages, building confidence is even more so.

Therefore, you should start to celebrate every small success. Make a note of them in a journal. You got a client booking today? Great, note that down. 20 people shared one of your blog posts on Facebook? That's progress. Your boss, or someone you respect, praised what you're doing? Make sure to record this achievement.

While none of these results, on their own, will enable you to make a living from your project, they represent stepping stones to that destination. For this reason, they must be acknowledged.

Of course, some people might say choosing to focus on the positives rather than the negatives (especially when the negatives outnumber the positives) is delusional but are they the keepers of the truth? Plenty of people have experienced years in the wilderness only to step into their success a decade after they started (legend has it that Colonel Sanders was rejected 1009 times before finding someone who was interested his chicken recipe – and he was well into his 60s at the time). Were they delusional for telling themselves they were making progress and sticking at it?

Ultimately, you are the one who gets to determine the truth (at least so far as it pertains to your success). Therefore, latch onto anything that helps and believe in anything that gives you permission to advance. You *will* grow. When you understand this, the fear of failing to meet your own expectations becomes manageable. In the early stages, your successes are what counts, not how far away you are from your goal.

CHAPTER 12: CLARITY WHEN YOU FEEL LIKE EVERYTHING IS LOST

There are few journeys as rewarding, yet as hard, as attempting to create the life you want. Achieving this goal means a life free from almost all societal conventions. You don't have a boss telling you what to do and you can set your own schedule. Furthermore, other people's opinions and judgements have zero effect on your decisions or self-esteem. In short, your life is untouched by the factors that seem to hold so many people back.

While living this way may sound ideal, it's what you have to give to get to this level that can take its toll. Every aspect of your character, and will, is going to be tested and, as a result, it's likely they'll be many occasions when you feel like giving up.

What you do in these moments will determine whether you get to live the life you want. When you feel like everything is lost, or what you're attempting to do is no longer feasible, it can be easy to look for alternatives. "Why don't I just go back living my old life?" you'll ask yourself. "Perhaps I could put up with a lack of fulfilment and excitement, it's better than losing it all," you'll say.

While this thinking is understandable, it overlooks the dissatisfaction that caused you to make this journey. The grass always appears greener when dealing with the demands of your present situation, but salvation isn't necessarily found through quitting. Instead, what you're going to need is a level head. Despite the inner turmoil you might be experiencing, you must find a way to detach from the emotion. Then, you can intelligently plan your next move.

The next three sections should help you achieve this state. They'll inform you on what to do when facing criticism of your plans, how to cope with crushing losses and the questions you must ask yourself if you ever feel like giving up. Combined, they should help you bounce back from your greatest challenges and give you a new lease of life.

Why you shouldn't listen to naysayers

In 2017, Mirjana Lucic-Baroni, a women's tennis player from Croatia, made the semi-final of the Australian Open singles competition. Remarkably, this was her first grand slam semi-final in almost 20 years.

Her professional tennis career started at the age of 15 and, only a year later, she reached the semi-finals of Wimbledon. At this point, she was destined to be the next big thing in women's tennis. However, instead of going on to win multiple grand slams and tens of millions of dollars in prizemoney, she retired at the unusually young age of 21, in 2003.

As is sometimes the case for young female tennis stars, she had a difficult relationship with her father. During her early years, she was physically abused and then, when she got older, had some of her prizemoney stolen. Eventually, she returned to the tennis tour in 2007 but never fulfilled her early promise.

Battling into her 30s, though, she had one final triumph with her semi-final place at the 2017 Australian Open. After achieving this success, and a much-needed career high pay day of $900,000, she had this to say about the many people who doubted she could relive her former glory, "Fuck everything and everybody who ever tells you, you can't do it. Just show up and do it with your heart."

You'll hear this kind of statement from a lot of famous sports stars who have succeeded against the odds. Unfortunately, with repetition, its power almost becomes hollow. However, in Mirjana's case, it's particularly poignant because of the struggles she endured to get back to this level.

First, were the expectations of her early career. Touted to be one of the top players of her generation, it would have been incredibly hard battling on into her 30s, against the disappointment of how her career played out.

Second, there were the demands of catching up with a game that may have left her behind. Four years is a long time out at the top of your profession. Having to recapture a level you competed at when a teenager must have been very demoralising.

While all this was going on, she would have had people whispering in her ear, telling her it was time to give up. By that stage, although probably not financially secure for the rest of her life, she'd have made some money from tennis and wouldn't have been in any immediate difficulty. Why not just take the easy way out and become a coach? Why put yourself through years of hard graft, training in the blazing sun and trying to remain competitive against younger opponents?

Ultimately, though, none of these factors would stop her. She had her heart set on reaching the top level of the game and the opinions of the naysayers didn't matter.

This is something you must learn. The opinions of other people can *never* stop you from being successful. Build a wall against them. As Mirjana says, "Fuck everything and everybody" who says you can't succeed. Perhaps some of them are your parents, Doctors or are so called experts in your industry. They might tell you to be cautious, that you're too old or that the world doesn't work the way you imagine. It doesn't matter. Nothing they say can have an impact on your success unless you allow their beliefs to become yours.

If you do listen to their opinions, you're opening yourself up to a world of hurt. Often, it's considered a flaw to charge ahead bullishly without being influenced by those around you. However, if you're constantly seeking the approval of others, or looking to avoid criticism, you will stymie yourself.

Of course, sometimes people can offer good advice and it needs to be heeded. You'll know the right time to seek feedback. On all other occasions, when people are trying to tear you down, warn you about supposed dangers and put fear into your mind, raise your protective wall and remind yourself that, you alone, will determine whether you succeed.

How to deal with heartbreak

Heartbreak can take many forms. Immediately, you might think about the loss of an important relationship. While this can be the most devastating type, you might also experience this emotion at the failure of an important project or when some unforeseen event comes in and turns your world turned upside down.

Such experiences can be incredibly derailing. Focus and motivation are wiped out in an instant. Months, if not years, of productive work can grind to a halt as you find yourself unable to attach any meaning to what has occurred. You may even feel like quitting or, if it's a romantic relationship, that you could never love again.

For these reasons, you need to know how to deal with heartbreak. I've experienced two throughout my life. Although it took me a long time to bounce back, the insights I learned should be invaluable in helping you move on from yours.

My first heartbreak happened at the age of 26. At this point in my life, I hadn't had a girlfriend, date or any kind of warmth or intimacy in seven very long years. However, my fortunes started to change as I began dating a girl who, initially, came to see me for tennis lessons.

It didn't take long before I fell in love. Her beauty, charm and my lack of romance for a very long time, formed a heady cocktail that enraptured my senses. I desperately wanted her to be my first, serious, girlfriend.

Despite the strength of my feelings, though, our romance was short lived. No sooner than we had started seeing each (a matter of weeks), she called it off.

There were complications with her ex, she told me. Apparently, she was still in love and wanted to give their relationship another try. I didn't understand. How, after so many years of rejection and loneliness, could I come so close to the love I longed for and then, suddenly, have it taken away? It felt like someone, or something, was playing a cruel joke on me.

It was no joke though. It was real and I had to accept it. The problem was, I didn't want to. I didn't want to focus on moving forwards. I'd lost my appetite for picking up the pieces and trying to make the best of the situation.

This was a heartbreak that took me many months, if not a year, to process. Despite our relationship being fleeting, I had invested so much, that I couldn't come to terms with its failure. I'd worked so hard to overcome my desperation and loneliness that, failure, at this point, was crushing.

As it turned out, though, the experience didn't break me. In fact, it taught me many lessons, primary amongst them was that obsessive love is unhealthy. Make one object, even if that object be a person very dear to you, the centre of your life, and you're heading for heartbreak.

The simple, and unfortunate, fact is that they could be taken away from you. If they're your children, they'll inevitably grow up and leave the family home. If they're your husband or wife, they might decide they don't love you anymore and leave. Whatever they are to you, tragically, there's always the potential they might die. Therefore, you must protect yourself *before the fact*.

Protecting yourself doesn't mean holding back and not giving 100% of your love. It certainly doesn't mean expecting something to go wrong so that, when it does, you'll feel prepared. Instead, it means entering into any relationship knowing that *you* are the source for your happiness and wellbeing, not the other person. Of course, you may love being around them and capture a feeling you simply can't get while on your own, but they can *never* become the source of your joy. That way lies the potential for heartbreak because what happens if your joy gets taken away?

When you find the source of your happiness from within, you are still affected by the loss of the people you love. Breakups will hurt and deaths will be tragic. However, you have your emotional anchor and, unfortunate, even tragic events won't permanently derail you.

Finding your happiness within is something you'll have to work on every day. There are so many external influences – food, drugs, sex, TV, other people, special events – vying for your attention and offering a quick boost to your energy. Without vigilance, it can be hard not to end up living for them.

The antidote is developing a greater awareness of your inner world. Throughout the day, you must be mindful of how you're thinking and feeling. Where's your energy at? Is it low? If so, raise it by focusing on feeling happy. You don't even have to attach a particular thought or outcome to the feeling. Instead, a conscious directive to raise your energy will be enough. The rest is hard work and practise.

This is your defence against heartbreak. Years of having performed this practise will ensure you can access your happiness when times get tough. You'll be able to recalibrate, even without the person who meant so much to you.

My second heartbreak occurred after the failure of my book (back in 2012). I've already discussed the events leading up to this experience and the impact it had on my psyche. To elaborate a little further, I was left dejected and with no appetite to continue in my quest to become a bestselling author.

It seemed life didn't care about how hard I'd worked. It didn't give a damn about how noble my intentions were either. The project I thought would transform my life couldn't even sell 100 copies in a year.

This heartbreak was incredibly demotivating. Yes, I continued working, attempting to build an audience for my work through a blog and a YouTube channel but, mentally, I couldn't give it my all. I was too hurt. I felt that the monumental effort I gave to write my book should have been enough to ensure success.

If you're ever faced with a similar heartbreak (giving everything you have to a project and it coming to nothing), then give yourself room to breathe and rest. Take a little time off. Once the disappointment has faded, try to understand that, hard work dedicated to a worthy cause, is rarely wasted.

Your project may, almost, be good enough. With a clear assessment of what needs to be improved (which can only be given when you can look at the project without emotion), you might be able to make some quick changes that bring you the level of success you desire.

Even if there are no quick fixes, you may find that your work can be repurposed. For example, your book may not have caught on, but can it be turned into a course? Or, your band failed to get a record deal or generate any interest, but can you use your insight into the industry to become a manager or band photographer? Be creative with your knowledge. Don't let the negative emotion of a heartbreak blind you from these opportunities.

One reaction you must never have with heartbreaks (of any kind) is losing your capacity to love or believe in good. The most powerful act of defiance you can take against the disappointments you've experienced is to say, *"You will not break me. You will not turn me into a twisted cynic or turn me away from the dreams I hold dear to my heart."*

This is the way you fight back. If you're mad, angry or upset, channel all your energy into becoming greater than before. Live, and love, harder than ever. Become so resilient, smart and desirable, that you limit the possibility of life's events going against you. Eventually, you'll find that the heart can heal from any wound and that love, and success, can be experienced again.

The 3 questions you must ask before giving up on your dreams

I've thought about giving up on many occasions. First, I wanted to quit tennis coaching when I realised that most lessons were more about controlling a bunch of rowdy kids than teaching them about a sport. Then, when I started working as a hypnotherapist, and would deliver, what I believed, was a perfect session and the client would surprise me by saying that nothing had changed, my thoughts would turn to giving up. I've even thought about giving up on my dream of becoming a best-selling author. After having spent years writing a book that, initially, no one was interested in, I found it too much to take.

Thoughts like,

- This is just too hard.
- Wouldn't it be so much easier if I just jacked it all in, used my degree and got myself a conventional job?
- Do all these failures mean I'm just not good enough?
- What am I sacrificing by continuing down this path which appears to have no end in sight? Might I miss out on the chance for love and happiness?

were to be found, at regular intervals, in my mind.

Perhaps you've felt the same. There's something you love doing, or that's really important for you to succeed at, but you don't seem to be making any progress. You've tried 100 different approaches but nothing has worked. As a result, you're starting to question yourself. You're beginning to wonder whether you're just not cut out for this particular journey.

Then, as you're going through this thought process, a painful feeling hits. It's one of loss. The thought of giving up on this thing you love so much, although seemingly inevitable, tears at your core. What do you do?

Some people will warn you against giving up too soon. They'll tell you persistence is the key and regale you with stories of people who succeeded decades after they originally started. Others will tell you to protect yourself. Trying to achieve something is fine but, when your attempts to succeed become obsessional and, therefore, unhealthy, you should stop.

Who's right? Do the persistence police have the answer or should you listen to the be reasonable brigade?

Ultimately, you must decide for yourself but, before you do, ponder the following three questions. Answering them will help you determine whether there's more left in the tank or whether it's time to call it a day.

The first question you must ask yourself when considering giving up on a dream or goal is, "what would I tell my child?" If you don't have one, imagine glimpsing into the future and having a meaningful conversation with your offspring.

In this conversation, your child looks to you for guidance. They're beginning to form ideas about what they want to do with their future and acquiring the ability to work towards a goal.

While doing so, it's inevitable that they'll struggle. No matter how much effort they put into their project, they might reach a plateau which they can't break through. What will you tell them?

Is it going to be, "Play it safe, don't expect too much or you'll be disappointed?" Or, is it going to be, "If you're passionate about doing something then you MUST pursue it and find every way possible to make it work?"

I'd be surprised if it was the first statement (otherwise why bother having kids). However, how rarely do we live up to our ideals?

This question is a perspective shifter. It places you outside your predicament and forces you to asks questions about what you want your legacy to be. Often the advice you would give another is the advice you should take yourself.

Look to the bigger picture. Sometimes success and failure are the wrong criteria for assessing whether you should continue. What about questions regarding the integrity of what you're doing? Is there a deeper reason you're so intensely involved in this project? Is it the right thing to do?

Answering these questions should snap you out of your funk and reconnect you with your *why*. Expect a massive burst of energy to follow. It could be so powerful that it pushes you to the next level on your project and enables you to make a breakthrough.

What if, though, when speaking to your imaginary (or real) child, you told them to "be realistic?" If this is the case, then perhaps you need some time out. Take a break, hang out with friends, take a vacation or start a new sport or hobby. Soon, you'll discover whether it was your goal that was making you miserable or whether you were just temporarily overwhelmed by the enormity of the task.

How will you know? You'll either be itching to get back into action or forgetting about it completely. With your answer, you can then plan your next move.

The next question you need to ask when considering giving up on a goal or dreams is, "Have I tried absolutely everything?" While this question may seem obvious, it's amazing how many people give up on something they love while still holding an ace up their sleeve. You have to exhaust *all* of your ideas (but not necessarily resources) before you can consider giving up.

Find a pen and paper and answer these questions to gain clarity,

- What contacts do I know, that might help further my cause, yet I haven't approached?
- What new business ideas (a new book, a new product line) do I feel really excited about but haven't created?
- What adjustments to my current business line could I make to increase sales and exposure?
- What's the one thing I'm really scared of doing, that I haven't done yet, but I know would have an impact?
- Is there some way I can improve my skill-set (going on a course, getting a mentor, working more hours) so that I become more proficient in my field?

When you can get through this entire list and come up with nothing (and only then), it might be time to quit and try something new. If you can find answers and, most importantly, are still in love with what you're doing, then you must continue.

A long-forgotten contact might share your work and open you up to a new audience. Starting a YouTube channel might be the thing that gets your work noticed. Simply working 5 more hours a week, on a consistent basis, might make you productive enough to build the momentum needed for a breakthrough.

Richard Branson echoed these thoughts in an interview with Seth Godin. Godin asked him what entrepreneurs should do when experiencing tough times and whether, at any point, they should quit. His advice was this,

> Do everything you can to survive and not to give up. As long as you've tried everything you can, then if you fail, you'll sleep ok and you'll pick yourself up and when things are better, you'll learn from your mistakes and start again. If, on the other hand, you give up too readily, you'll forever kick yourself. [38]

The final question you need to ask when considering giving up on your dreams is, "Why do I want to succeed?" What is driving you to put so much into this endeavour? Is it the money? Perhaps it's the potential to be famous, respected or loved? Maybe you seek power or want to make a difference?

I would suggest that, when you look at the deeper motives driving you towards success, what lies behind them is the simple desire to feel good. Nothing else. You have an idea or vision of how great life will be *once* you've achieved your goal, and you pursue this idea or vision with the belief that its attainment will make you feel that way permanently. Therefore, your primary drive is to feel amazing. However, when you understand that you don't need to achieve a goal to feel this way, everything changes.

The good news is that you can feel great independent of any external stimulus. With training, you can raise your energy through your thoughts alone. All it takes is awareness of how you feel and the repeated mental instruction to feel good.

Therefore, you don't need your goal to fill a hole. You can do it all by yourself.

With this knowledge, your perspective changes. Presently, you may be working incredibly hard and feeling burned out. If that's the case, take a step back and take some time off. Instead of working on your project, work on feeling good. Train yourself to find your happiness and joy from within. Once you make sufficient progress with this, ask yourself how you feel about giving up.

Are you still inspired by your project? If so, then continue. It's likely that the time off, and training in raising your energy, will give you new ideas, or lead to a new approach, that enables you to make a breakthrough.

What happens, though, if, after this time off, you're no longer inspired by your project? If this is the case, it's likely you were using your project as a vehicle. You imagined that, at some point in the future, it was going to bring you wealth, love or whatever it was that you desired. However, the reality of getting to this point was not enjoyable.

Furthermore, you've now discovered you don't need wealth, love or whatever you desire to feel good. Therefore, you can walk away from your project and still be ok.

Also, it's likely that, if you've been working on raising your energy, you'll come up with new ideas for projects to pursue, or a so-called chance encounter will lead you to a new opportunity. Inspiration opens doors so don't be afraid to let the old one shut.

One thing you must remember, though, is that you can *never* give up on your quest for happiness. This is a nonnegotiable. It is more important than any material reward you'll achieve and must be worked on every day.

Hopefully, you're now ready to reassess your journey. The three questions we explored will help you determine whether greater persistence is required, whether you've exhausted all your options and whether, with a correct understanding of why you're pursuing your goal, it's still viable.

Personally, I'm very pleased I didn't give up on my dreams. I've had a positive impact on people's lives, had some enjoyable experiences and, most important of all, *proved* to myself that no obstacle is too difficult to overcome. None of this would have happened if I'd given up. What might you achieve if you stick at it a little longer?

CONCLUSION: THE 5 STEPS TO FREEDOM

This book is a departure from my previous two. Rather than having one consistent theme running from cover to cover, it deals with a lot of different areas that, once combined, provide the complete picture on creating the life you want.

As a result of this difference, a conclusion which ran along traditional lines, and provided you with an inspirational send-off, might have been out of place. While my previous books concluded by referencing life changing movies and evoking ground breaking voyages, this one will follow a different tack. I'm going to provide you with something more practical but no less profound.

This book contains 12 different chapters and 47 different sub-sections. There's a lot of information to digest. Perhaps there's a risk of information overload and, with that in mind, I've designed a uniquely useful conclusion.

What you are about to read is the distilled wisdom of the entire book. In 5 easy to understand, and chronological, steps, you'll have the next two to five years of your life mapped out.

My recommendation is that you download and print an extended PDF version (click this link to obtain www.escapethesystemnow.com/10steps) of this conclusion so that you can keep it separately. Rely on it as both a reminder of the practical steps you need to take and the mind-set necessary to succeed. Reread it monthly. As the lessons sink in, and you adjust your life to their dictates, powerful changes will occur.

Here's your roadmap to greatness.

Step Number 1: Understand that there is no easy path through life

You may have already questioned, or at this very moment, be questioning, your decision to break free from a regular life and pursue the life of your dreams. Sometimes, it can seem crazy. By your own volition, you're going to earn less money (at least initially), invite the possibility of ridicule and rejection and increase your chances of experiencing failure. Who would do such a thing?

Added to this, is the fact there's no guarantee of success. You're following an idea. You *think* you might succeed at whatever has captivated your attention. Or, maybe, at best, you *believe*.

Is that enough? What happens when your journey begins, or deepens, and that belief gets tested?

At this point, you may realise you no longer have the security of the system to rely on. In the reality you now operate (forging your own path), it's no longer a case of following the rules, doing what everybody else does and hoping your life will turn out ok. Instead, you face the potential of disaster if it all goes wrong (or at least this is what society will tell you).

All of these factors might fill your mind with doubt. When getting started, or at the most difficult points in your journey, you might wonder about what you've given up.

It's very easy, when looking in from the outside, to think that you're missing out. You might see former colleagues with steady jobs, some of them getting paid a large salary, and resent the fact you're scrimping and saving. You might hear about weddings and the birth of a first child and feel like you could be giving up on your chance for love and a family. You might look at friends and family members, all living a conventional life, and imagine their minds are devoid of turmoil while yours is filled with uncertainty and angst. Everything seems easier when you follow the crowd. But is it?

At this point, you must remember why a regular life was never enough for you. Remember all the travel, the endless working hours and the pointless meetings. Remember feeling the emptiness of working for nothing more than a monthly pay check. Remember all the bullshitting. Whether it was fake enthusiasm for your job, excessive drinking or partying so you could "fit in" or denying your true interests, ideas and passions, it was hard to maintain. Finally, remember the damage to your health and vitality this lifestyle caused. You'd had enough, right?

So, why, just because you've experienced walking your own path and found that it's not as easy as you imagined, do you think the life you used to live will be any different than before? Sure, it might provide a reprieve for 6 months but, after a while, won't all of the old frustrations resurface?

What's the lesson?

There is no easy path. Whether walking your own or following society's, both involve hardship, sacrifice and struggle, just of a very different kind.

So, what are you going to do?

When both paths offer their own degree of difficulty, you must look to the potential payoff. Here, there's a marked difference. At best, society's path offers comfort and security. However, being successful at creating the life you want is the route to freedom, love and meaning.

Which will you choose? Be aware that this is a decision you might have to make at multiple stages throughout your journey. Of course, it's made at the start but there will be times within the first few years, and beyond, when turning back will seem more appealing.

On each occasion, repeat the thought process above. It will steady your ship and remind you that there is no easy way out, just one way through.

Step number 2: Don't think like everybody else

Most of us are born with similar capabilities. A functioning brain, nervous system and two arms and legs are given to almost all. Therefore, what sets us apart? Why is it that one individual can climb the peaks of achievement and separate themselves from the masses, while the other appears ordinary and fails to achieve their ambitions?

While many point to genetic inheritance, this only explains a small piece of the puzzle. The true answer is to be found in the mind. If you want to excel, if you want to live your wildest dreams, you can't think like everybody else.

Why is this important? Most people get trapped into believing in the "real world." As a result, they think life can only be one way and that we are all living a shared, universal experience.

In this experience, there are written, and unwritten, rules that govern our behaviour and possibilities. Dreams rarely come true, it's not possible to be happy all of the time and only the exceptionally talented or lucky get to live extraordinary lives. This is the "real world." We may not like this reality, but we have to accept it. Life couldn't be any different.

The problem with this type of thinking is the limitation it imposes on your life. You simply can't excel, or live a different life, if you accept the "real world." Your efforts will be blocked at every turn because of one simple belief - *ordinary people don't live remarkable lives*. As a result, you'll shut yourself down. Even if you have a great idea, or are impressively skilled, you will talk yourself out of fulfilling your potential because the mass mind-set tells you it can't be done.

Right now, you must stop thinking like everybody else. Place no limits on what you can do. Dare to see possibilities that other people wouldn't even consider. Stretch your thinking beyond your so-called race, culture, religion, nationality and time.

Do this, and you'll start to reconnect with your genius and inspiration. From there, anything is possible.

Step Number 3: Make your goal/what you want to become, your dominant daily thought

You spend most of your conscious, waking hours, thinking. While most people never appreciate or understand the power contained in these moments, you must approach your mental activity differently. Every single thought is an opportunity to advance.

Of course, not every single thought can be controlled. There will be vast swathes of time when you need to focus on the task at hand and moments when you need to relax. However, for every other occasion, you must begin the habit of directing your thoughts towards your purpose.

This means that when washing dishes, cleaning up, walking, showering, travelling and while engaged in any other relatively mundane activity, you'll be thinking about what you want to achieve, or who you want to become.

Of course, this directive comes with the pre-requisite that you have ascertained your life's purpose. You must be clear on what it is you want to do. If you haven't found out what that is yet, don't worry. Pick something, anything. So long as it's positive, and its achievement will bring you happiness and fulfilment, this is enough to get started.

Then, focus your mind. You can always change your objective as you grow, but you can't relax your mental discipline. Become obsessed. Society will warn you about reaching this level, but it's by harnessing the power of your mind that you'll receive the insights, and experience the so-called chance encounters, that light a path to the life you want.

Step number 4: Focus on your successes, don't dwell on your failures

On your journey to creating the life you want, it's likely that your failures will outweigh your success by a ratio of ten to one. Understandably, this can be disheartening. Especially in the early stages, when you're constantly being rejected or ignored, this dejection could cause you to consider giving up.

To prevent this from happening, you must undergo a shift in mind-set. Rather than dwelling on your more frequent failures, you must learn to focus on the successes.

Of course, such a shift doesn't mean that you ignore your failures. You must still learn from them and use the experience as a way of gaining feedback. However, after having absorbed the lesson, your failures can't be given any further space in your mind.

You may wonder what an acceptable length of time is when it comes processing, and then letting go of, your failures. Being impacted for an hour is understandable. Perhaps, if it's been a particularly heavy blow, the rest of the day can be written off. However, when you wake the next day, that failure must be cast out of your mind.

Choose to focus on your achievements. Yes, you may have failed to secure an important deal, but what happened last week? Clients raved about your work and emailed to let you know about the positive impact you're having. This is what you need to focus on.

Routinely engaging in this practise will hit a switch in your mind. With time, the setbacks won't sting as much. In fact, they might be so temporary that it's only a matter of minutes before you're back to thinking about where your next success will come from.

Ultimately, this increases the energy you bring to your quest. Reacting to failure brings you down. Focusing on success keeps you motivated. Other people may tell you that you're deluding yourself by living this way but what purpose does it serve to feel demoralised by defeat?

You've already made up your mind that you are going to be successful at creating the life you want. You're thinking about it every day. Take the next step and *choose* to focus on the progress you're making.

Step number 5: Work a minimum of 20 hours a week on your passion

At present, you may have a full-time job. You may even have family commitments. However, you will still need to make time to work on your passion.

Without committing 20 hours a week to a project that will enable you to live the life you want, it's difficult to build momentum. Contacts must be made, products created and skills developed. This all takes time. Perhaps more time than you think.

If you approach these tasks with the attitude that you'll work on them when you get the chance, little will be accomplished. You won't follow up quickly enough with a potential client and lose their business. You'll miss your product launch date. Or, you simply won't get good enough at a skill to be able to make money from it. This is what happens when you work 5 hours a week on your passion one week, 30 the next and nothing at all on the week after that. However, if you have a well thought out schedule and regularly put in 20-hour weeks, important changes occur.

Of course, if you have more time at your disposal, or have recently quit your job to work exclusively on your project, you can invest up to or even over, 40 hours a week. However, what happens if you don't have this luxury?

You must become a master at time management. From week to week, you must know when you'll be able to do your 20 hours.

Do you have an hour before work available? Is it possible to work on your project while commuting? If working from home, is there time, while unsupervised, that you could dedicate to your working on your project instead of your day job? What have you got planned at the weekend? Amongst potential family commitments and having fun, where will you find 5 or 10 hours?

It's a struggle. There's no way to sugar coat this aspect of creating the life you want. Added to the mental discipline of channelling your thoughts, you must find time to work on a project when you're tired, demotivated, aggravating a boyfriend or girlfriend, husband or wife (they might say it's taking time away from the relationship) and struggling against the tide of failure. However, persist you must, because something incredible occurs when you keep putting in the hours.

You improve. Don't underestimate the amazing capacity you have to learn and grow. At present, you may look at what you want to accomplish and feel like you're being asked to climb Mount Everest. However, with two or three years of consistently working 20 hours a week on your project, the landscape completely alters.

You become a different person. Now, because you know your industry inside out, you can see all the opportunities that exist. Furthermore, because your skills are finely honed and you've built up a network of contacts, you're in a position to take advantage of them. This kind of experience only comes with thousands of hours invested in your project. Put the work in and you *will* see the results.

* * * * *

I hope you've found these steps, and this book, useful. If you want to continue your reading and discover the complete 10 steps to freedom, then please head over to www.escapethesystemnow.com/10steps and download, your *free* PDF today. The steps above will be included, alongside an additional five, in their original chronological order.

Make use of this resource. Refer to it regularly. It will provide all the clarity and direction you need to advance in your journey.

Above all, though, believe in yourself. There is no power outside of your own mind that can stop you from being successful. Move forwards boldly. A new life can be yours.

YOUR FREE GIFT

As a thank you for purchasing and reading *The Personal Freedom Manifesto* I want to give you a gift. Head over to www.escapethesystemnow.com/landing to claim your copy of the *30 Days to Escape The System* course. Download and you will learn;

- How to make a living from your passion.
- The 2 things you need to be successful doing it.
- How to overcome the inevitable adversity that every entrepreneur, world changer and dreamer will face.
- How to free yourself from fears, worries and hang ups.
- The 5 challenges you must complete to build the foundations of your new life.

Further Reading

If you enjoyed, *The Personal Freedom Manifesto*, you might be interested in my previous two books. The first, with over 120 five-star reviews on Amazon, is *Escape The System*.

Break the rules to get the life you want!

"A brilliant brilliant read, written really well, and really easy to follow. It's interesting, and engaging, the examples are great. I think it's life changing."
- **Danica Apolline**

"This book is a finely crafted masterpiece of personal development. It is actually the best I have ever read."
- **Tom Banner**

Buy the book by entering this link online
http://mybook.to/JoeEscape

Do The Work you Love

My second book, released in 2020 through Watkins Media.

Never work a boring job again!

"Well-structured and defined - an excellent approach to getting the best out of what you have. Thoroughly recommend."

- Henry Jamieson

"This book is really well written. It's a good advice book with practical options for someone who may be looking to escape the 9-5 40hrs a week slog."

- Miss Rose

> Buy the book by entering the link online
> http://mybook.to/Do_work_you_love

But that's not all . . .

Want to become a part of a vibrant, supportive online and "in person" community? Sign up to Success Club and receive monthly meet ups offering inspiring talks and a chance to meet like-minded people.

Search "Success Club" on meetup.com or follow this link https://www.meetup.com/meetup-group-bIxeHMnE

COACHING

Are you serious about creating the life you want? If so, then why not speed up the process by having me coach you? Email me at joe@escapethesystemnow.com to arrange a FREE consultation. This can be done at your convenience and typically takes place via Skype or Zoom.

Let me know what you're struggling with and I'll explain how I can help. Furthermore, if you quote "Freedom" in the subject bar when you send the email, I'll give you a 25% discount off the first session should you decide to book.

I can help you;

- Gain clarity on your present situation so you are clear about what you are working, and living, towards.
- Discover a passion, or fine tune any of the ideas you currently have.
- Develop a clear plan so you know what the next 3 to 6 months of your life will look like, how much work you are going to do and where you'll find the time to do it.
- Remove any anxiety or fear that's been holding you back.
- Introduce new habits that'll ensure you get the most out of every day.
- Find previously hidden levels of motivation and confidence.
- Remain accountable to any schedule, and actions, we agree on.

I've been coaching clients in multiple fields for over 15 years. In 2003, I qualified as a tennis coach and went on to train players who have reached national level. In 2005, I qualified as a hypnotherapist and, to this day, help clients overcome lifelong bad habits, break free from crippling anxieties and enhance their well-being through improved sleep and the reduction of stress. Finally, since 2015, I've been coaching readers of my books to find, and succeed at, doing the work they love.

Due to my varied experience, I'm skilled in a variety of techniques to help you unluck your potential and achieve your aim. Whether it's hypnotherapy, NLP, cutting edge coaching tools or some my own techniques that I've honed through over 15 years of experience, I'll find a way to help you towards your next breakthrough. Email me today at joe@escapethesystemnow.com to arrange your FREE consultation.

Testimonials from clients:

"Joe helped me tremendously transform into the person I was meant to be. He is kind, patient and has a profound understanding of deep blockages of the mind. For years I was struggling to achieve my goals and overcome my limiting beliefs. Now I am in a much better position at work, while accomplishing a life of financial and location freedom as a physician and musician."

- Dr. Khalid

"I was first introduced to Joe through his book "Do the work you Love." The book gave me the confidence to take a serious look at running my own business. After I read the book, I followed the link and contacted Joe. He was so approachable and an amazing mentor. Without you, I would be back in the system and at the grind stone. With you I am free and happy."

- Allan L.

ACKNOWLEDGEMENTS

To everyone who has bought and reviewed a copy of *Escape The System* or *Do The Work you Love*. It's hugely appreciated.

To Chucri Chelhot for his proof reading and support.

To all Success Club members. I love the community we've created and it's great to see you all succeeding with your own projects.

To Claire Daly for your love and support.

ENDNOTES

[1] Aviva Study, "Sleepless cities revealed as one in three adults suffer from insomnia." https://www.aviva.com/newsroom/news-releases/2017/10/Sleepless-cities-revealed-as-one-in-three-adults-suffer-from-insomnia/

[2] Susie Steiner, "Top Five Regrets of the Dying".https://www.theguardian.com/lifeandstyle/2012/feb/01/top-five-regrets-of-the-dying

[3] Steve Doughty, "Britons spend an average of 42 Hours at work each week – more than anyone else in Europe". https://www.bbc.co.uk/news/uk-politics-49795179

[4] Susan Adams, "New Survey: Majority of Employees Dissatisfied". https://www.forbes.com/sites/susanadams/2012/05/18/new-survey-majority-of-employees-dissatisfied/#5932f804663c

[5] Kedar Grandhi, "Coca-Cola pays millions to hide obesity claims". https://www.ibtimes.co.uk/coca-cola-pays-millions-counter-obesity-claims-1523193

[6] Bruce H. Lipton, *The Biology of Belief*, Hay House, INC. 2015.

[7] Thomas Kuhn, *The Structure of Scientific Revolutions*, University of Chicago Press, 1962.

[8] Kashmira Gander, "Being lazy could be genetic say scientists".
https://www.independent.co.uk/news/science/being-lazy-could-be-genetic-say-scientists-9128595.html

[9] Frank Lucas, *Original Gang$ter,* Ebury Press, 2010.

[10] Jim Clifton, "The World's Broken Workplace".
https://news.gallup.com/opinion/chairman/212045/world-broken-workplace.aspx?g_source=position1&g_medium=related&g_campaign=tiles

[11] James Salmon, "I totally f***** with the Palo market today': Damning emails of Barclays traders boasting about how they rigged energy prices to make profits".
https://www.dailymail.co.uk/news/article-2226592/Barclays-traders-damned-emails-reveal-bragged-rigging-energy-prices-make-profits.html

[12] P Butterworth, "The psychosocial quality of work determines whether employment has benefits for mental health: results from a longitudinal national household panel survey."
https://oem.bmj.com/content/68/11/806.abstract

[13] Glassdoor Survey, "More than half of employees would stay longer at their company if their bosses showed more appreciation". https://www.glassdoor.com/about-us/employees-stay-longer-company-bosses-showed-appreciation-glassdoor-survey/

[14] Jon Morrow, "How to Quit your Job, move to Paradise and Get Paid to Change the World". https://problogger.com/how-to-quit-your-job-move-to-paradise-and-get-paid-to-change-the-world/?inf_contact_key=28b979d4942d5b4dc1e46ebd4f098d07b3a86f68fb4b2a080bdd535b44d22ddd

[15] James Davies, Cracked, Icon Books LTD, 2013.

[16] Neringa Antanaityte, "Mind Matters: How to effortlessly have more positive thoughts". https://tlexinstitute.com/how-to-effortlessly-have-more-positive-thoughts/

[17] Maxwell Maltz, *Psycho-Cybernetics,* Pocket, 1960.

[18] Annie Murphy Paul, "Self-Help: Shattering the Myths". https://www.psychologytoday.com/gb/articles/200103/self-help-shattering-the-myths

[19] Conrad Black, "Review: Bonaparte by Patrice Gueniffey". http://www.conradmblack.com/1117/review-bonaparte-by-patrice-gueniffey

[20] Arnold Schwarzenegger, *Total Recall,* Simon and Schuster, 2013.

[21] Brian Mattimore, *21 Days to a Big Idea!,* Diversion Books, 2015.

[22] Microdot, "NLP Communication Model". http://www.microdot.net/nlp/learning-strategy/communication-model.shtml

[23] Muhamad Hamim Bin Abdul Rahim, *Chasing the Elusive Work-Life Balance for the Working Singaporean,* Partridge Publishing Singapore, 2014.

[24] Bruce Thomas, *Bruce Lee Fighting Spirit,* Blue Snake Books, 1994.

[25] Tony Robbins, "What Drives your Decisions?" https://www.tonyrobbins.com/mind-meaning/what-drives-your-decisions/

[26] Nick Morgan, "Thinking of Self-Publishing your Book in 2013? Here's what you need to know". https://www.forbes.com/sites/nickmorgan/2013/01/08/thinking-of-self-publishing-your-book-in-2013-heres-what-you-need-to-know/#bf8468f14bb8

[27] Peter Edwards, "Hurricane Carter's Deathbed Plea: Ex-Boxer Battles for Release of New York Convict".
https://www.thestar.com/news/gta/2014/02/23/hurricane_carters_deathbed_plea_exboxer_battles_for_release_of_new_york_convict.html

[28] Ian Fleming, *Dr. No,* Thomas and Mercer, 2012.

[29] Sophie Austin, "What's the Average Salary in the UK?"
https://www.findcourses.co.uk/inspiration/articles/average-salary-uk-2018-14105

[30] FIFPro World Player's Union, "2016 FIFPro Global Employment Report".
https://www.fifpro.org/media/xdjhlwb0/working-conditions-in-professional-football.pdf

[31] Neringa Antanaityte, "Mind Matters: How to effortlessly have more positive thoughts". https://tlexinstitute.com/how-to-effortlessly-have-more-positive-thoughts/

[32] Boston College, "Trust your Gut: Intuitive decision making based on expertise may deliver better results than analytical approach".
https://www.sciencedaily.com/releases/2012/12/121220144155.htm

[33] The Sunday Times Magazine, "What I've Learned: Rene Redzepi". 24th May 2014

[34] Hugh McIlvanney, "Hugh McIlvanney on the most compelling figure in the history of sport".
https://www.thetimes.co.uk/article/the-man-who-shook-up-the-world-7zpxq2s66

[35] Viktor E Frankl, *Man's Search for Meaning,* Rider, 2004.

[36] Sue Quinn, "Number of Vegans in Britain rises 360% in 10 years". https://www.telegraph.co.uk/food-and-drink/news/number-of-vegans-in-britain-rises-by-360-in-10-years/

[37] Rob Knight, "Average Britain spends almost 10 years of their life watching TV, research finds".
https://www.independent.co.uk/news/media/tv-radio/average-watching-tv-briton-10-years-life-research-a8367526.html

[38] Richard Branson: Learning from Failure
https://www.youtube.com/watch?time_continue=15&v=S_3Dj5GZJNc&feature=emb_logo

Printed in Great Britain
by Amazon